Animals and Animal Dreams III

Cow, Octopus, and Snake

A Contribution from Depth Psychology

by Regina Abt-Baechi

translated by Alison Kappes

LIVING HUMAN HERITAGE PUBLICATIONS, ZURICH
2025

Frontispiece:
Uraeus-snake with horns of cow. 19th dynasty.
Valley of Queens, tomb of Nefertari.

Living Human Heritage Publications
Münsterhof 16, 8001 Zurich, Switzerland

info@livinghumanheritage.org
www.livinghumanheritage.org

ISBN-13 978-3-9525713-4-7

Layout: Tuğba Çetin and Theodor Abt

Print:
MAS Matbaacılık San. ve Tic. A.Ş.
Hamidiye Mahallesi, Soğuksu Caddesi No:3
34408 Kağıthane, İstanbul / Turkey
T. +90 212 294 10 00 (pbx) F. +90 212 294 90 80
book@masmat.com.tr Certificate No: 44686

Table of Contents

Acknowledgements 7
Introduction 9

1. The Cow 13
   Dream 1: On driving a car and the white cows 16
   Dream 2: The little red cow in the water 21
   Dream 3: The cow that gave birth 27
   Dream 4: The statue of Hathor in the Museum of Ancient History 37
   Dream 5: The ox-child 44

2. The Octopus 65
   Dream 6: The two octopuses in the sea 68
   Dream 7: The octopus/crab in prison 81

3. The Snake 87
   Dream 8: The black-and-white snake 90
   Dream 9: The copper-coloured snake 94
   Dream 10: The child and the *Boa constrictor* 100
   Dream 11: "Cutting up" a snake 106
   Dream 12: The captive snake 107
   Dream 13: The "redeemer snake" 111
   Dream 14: Snakes in the house 118
   Dream 15: The green snakes in the pond 126
   Dream 16: The rattlesnake entwined around the leg 132
   Dream 17: A viper (common European viper) winds its way around me 139
   Dream 18: The black cobra snake 155

4. Appendix 167
   1. Bibliography 169
   2. List of figures 174
   3. List of dreams 177
   4. Index 178

Acknowledgements

After Animal Dreams I on "The Cat, The Dog, and The Horse" and Animal Dreams II on 'The Fish,' in this volume, Animal Dreams III, perhaps "Cow, Octopus, and Snake" represent a surprising constellation. Once again, this work is based on important dreams that I owe to analysts, friends, and acquaintances. My thanks as ever go to my husband Theodor Abt, whose support and work on the text, layout, and printing made this book possible in the first place. I would also like to thank Sabine Mayer-Patzel for her valuable work on proofreading and index and Tuğba Çetin for the layout. And of course, my great thanks go to Alison Kappes for her excellent translation.

Spring 2025 Regina Abt-Baechi

"One beholds something really divine just in the eyes of the animals, for one sees there the expression of the creative will and the creative spirit."

C. G. Jung, *The Visions Seminars* I, p. 468.

Introduction

One might ask why we even bother to interpret dreams of people we may not know well? Dreams fascinate me because they speak of our inner nature, of the unconscious background of our thoughts, our actions, and our lives. If we try hard to understand the symbolic language of dreams, it is because it expresses a natural kind of knowledge that exceeds our own, one that can make life richer, more colourful, and more interesting. What Marie-Louise von Franz says about fairy tale interpretation also applies to dreams: «Psychological interpretation is our way of telling stories; we still have the same need, and we still crave the renewal that comes from understanding archetypal images.»[1] Perhaps, then, this book is simply a further attempt to tell some stories!

In the final article he wrote shortly before his death, C. G. Jung explains why we need to understand the importance of dream symbols: «For the sake of mental stability and even physiological health, the unconscious and the conscious must be integrally connected and thus move on parallel lines. If they are split apart or 'dissociated,' psychological disturbance follows. In this respect, dream symbols are the essential message carriers from the instinctive to the rational parts of the human mind, and their interpretation enriches the poverty of consciousness so that it learns to understand again the forgotten language of the instincts.»[2]

What, then, do animals and our instincts have in common? Animals act largely instinctively, according to their innate behavioural patterns: dogs usually run when a rabbit crosses their path; cats sit for hours in front of mouse holes; spiders always weave the same webs; birds fly across entire continents to their breeding grounds. This is instinctive behaviour that serves life, and it can be found in humans, too. But because we readily

1 M.-L. von Franz, *Interpretation of Fairy Tales*, p. 45.

2 C. G. Jung, *Man and his Symbols*, p. 52.

assume that we already know how we behave, we seldom realize that we have, as Jung says, forgotten the language of our instincts. It makes sense, then, to engage with dreams about animals. They can provide us in pictorial form with fairly accurate descriptions of how things work in the unconscious world of our 'animal' instincts![3]

Dreams that bring up general and fundamental things from the deeper layers of the human psyche seem more meaningful than others. If we manage to grasp the meaning of their symbolic language, dreams compensate and complement in a holistic sense the limited and often ill-adapted state of our consciousness.[4] We refer to these dreams as archetypal dreams and they form the subject matter of this book. While not completely omitting the personal aspects of the dreamer, we do not, however, provide case studies or psychological prescriptions. No two dreams ever have the same meaning. "Wat den eenen sin Uhl, is den annern sin Nachtigall", as a north German idiom says (what is for one an owl is for another a nightingale). [The equivalent in English might be "One man's meat is another man's poison."] The same dream image can have a different meaning for different people. Our focus is therefore upon the archetypal symbols that belong, as it were, to the shared human substratum of the unconscious psyche. By surpassing all that we know thus far, archetypal symbols provide us with a much broader dimension in which to understand human behaviour across all language, religious, and cultural boundaries.

Despite globalization, the polarity of the opposites is becoming more intense in our time: belligerent tones, ideological trench warfare and bellicose confrontations dominate media and political events, making any 'understanding' unpopular. Thus, finding common ground that makes understanding possible in the first place is of the utmost importance.

3 B. Hannah, *The Archetypal Symbolism of Animals.* This book gives the best and most detailed summary of animal symbolism: based on Jungian insights and using rich material, the author amplifies and presents the symbolic meaning of the dog, the horse, the cat, the snake, and the lion.

4 See C. G. Jung, *Alchemical Studies,* [CW 13], § 397.

Many who have had little exposure to Jung like to see both him and his research as being somewhat unfashionable, already outdated, from the last century, as it were. Our modern Zeitgeist is heading in a different direction, toward new and seemingly ever-improved insights. To the best of my knowledge, however, no psychology, philosophy, or other school of thought has, until now, not only explored the realm of the unconscious in its entire intellectual-historical reach, but also provided us with a method of understanding unconscious imagery and its effect on the human being, better than Jung. As Laurens van der Post once meaningfully quipped in a lecture, "We are not ahead of him, we are still trying to catch up to him." By this he meant that we are still far from grasping the full scope and significance for our time of this completely new understanding of the human species that Jung brought into the light of consciousness.

In what follows, we will be approaching step by step some aspects of our unconscious instinctual nature as it appears in dreams. But why the cow, the octopus, and the snake? I admit it is a somewhat strange selection. At the beginning of each chapter, I try to describe what prompted my choice. But, at bottom, I do not know what teasing spirit pointed my nose in their direction and motivated me to tackle this third book on dreams about animals.[5]

5 R. Abt-Baechi, *Animals and Animal Dreams. The Cat, the Dog, and the Horse.* And: R. Abt-Baechi, *Animals and Animal Dreams II, The Fish.*

Part I

The Cow

Fig. 1: Cow of the breed ‘Original Brown’ in the field.

When I walk past cows and they look at me with their still, dark eyes, I find myself compelled to stop. They induce me to stand quite still, as still as they are. After being milked in the barn in the early hours of the morning and ambling slowly in a long line to the pasture, they then stand or lie in the grass, eating or resting, and chewing their cud. Now and then they groom each other, licking each other's head, neck, and face, deliberately, in prolonged repetition, and, as if not to miss any of this pleasant grooming and massage, the one being treated thus remains devotedly still. Dignified and weighty, the bull moves among his herd as he pleases, diligently assessing the affection and willingness of his females. Whether or not he is the undisputed master of the herd, I do not know. Although he is, with all his stubborn violence, a monument of creative power, I suspect that there are those among the cows who play a more important role in the coexistence of the herd than he does. As I approach him – from the other side of the fence, of course – he fixes his eyes upon me, and takes a few steps toward me or along the line of fence. Sometimes he snorts or strikes the soft earth with a foreleg in warning. I recall that his predecessor used to stab deep holes in the ground whenever he got excited. This one is calmer and eventually turns away to rejoin the cows. Why do these animals, that can play, fight, and gallop around with swinging udders in their awkward, lumbering way, give me such a deep sense of calm? Something in me responds to them, is like them, and that is why I become still when I stand next to them.

For as long as there have been domesticated cattle, many people must have had a feeling like my own today. Our ancestors had a different relationship to these animals. For them, cattle were spirited beings with their own mind with whom they lived at close quarters and had to do deal with to survive. Cattle were the basis of their sustenance, and, in certain cultures, their milk was considered a drink of the gods. Their relationship to their cattle was closer, more down-to-earth. The cows and calves we deal with are mostly packaged in plastic in supermarkets, and their milk in Tetra Pak or in a bottle, not to mention the injustice we do to these living creatures with our inhumane conditions of industrial meat production and the misery inherent in cattle transportation.

So, what does all of this have to do with our topic of studying this animal in our dreams? As if seen on slate or on a prehistoric cave wall, the image of the cow has been carved into the human psyche – an image we still hold today. When we encounter this image in a dream, it seems to affect us in a strange way. In dreams, we are given a glimpse of something going on in our psyche where cow and bull each play their own distinctive role.

To put distance between us and the beef steak in the supermarket, and to help us understand these images, we need to look back at what man has thought or said about this animal throughout the ages. By collecting this information, we will approach the deeper meaning behind the image of a cow, a bull, a calf, or any animal in a dream.[6]

After this first step has been taken, we must then, in the analytical hour, also consider the personal experiences, thoughts, and ideas of the dreamer. In this way, what the dream might mean for this person's life and what consequences might have to be drawn from it can slowly emerge.

A dream I heard a long time ago comes to mind, and here is a summary of it:

Dream 1: On driving a car and the white cows

The dreamer is driving a car on a rather dangerous road through hilly countryside. She is driving on the mountain side of the road at a brisk pace when suddenly two white cows appear in front of her. They are lying on the road, watched over by a woman. Not wanting to be delayed, the dreamer overtakes the cows and the woman without slowing down on the left-hand side of the road. Suddenly, she notices that this side of the road drops away steeply on the left. She drives on regardless, thinking that her car will manage. But it slides off to the left, down the embankment towards the bushes further down the slope. The dreamer wakes up in shock!

6 According to C. G. Jung, we call this method of illuminating dream images 'amplification,' meaning 'elucidation': we consider meaningfully related material, especially from comparative religious history, but also from popular narrative culture, such as fairy tales and legends.

The woman who had this dream rightly perceived it as a warning to reduce her speed, to assess her situation more realistically, and to respect the white cows and the woman. Clearly, the fast car and the resting cows provide a contrast to each other.

The dreamer doesn't want to be stopped: "I'll be fine", "no time" etc. Recklessly overestimating herself or misjudging the situation, she thinks she can get out of the way and not let either the cows or the woman slow her down. This makes her veer off the road. The car can represent the powerful, dynamic energy with which you move through life, and which gives you a certain independence and assertiveness. Here, however, this dynamic energy leads involuntarily and unconsciously to reckless speeding. As Jung showed, the unconscious of a woman has masculine overtones. He called this embodiment of the opposite-sex in the unconscious of women the animus. In male psychology, its equivalent is the anima. Both animus and anima can be positive or negative. Thus, in a simple way, this little dream shows that when a woman's unconscious, or animus, is driving the car, the feminine can be at risk. It reveals how dangerous it is when the animus influences our 'motivation' (movere: to drive, to move), or our 'motives'.

If we look carefully at this approach in women, we often see that the dynamic energy of the car that is being influenced by the negative animus generates annoyance and a reckless lack of focus; these women become the mouthpiece of their own and other people's opinions and harbour stubborn, indisputable convictions.[7] This energy is not even remotely that of the 'helpful motor' that enriches life: instead, it drives one 'offside'; it isolates or even drives one into conflict or depression. In our dream, this would be the motif of the car slipping down to the bottom left-hand side of the slope.

If the animus makes a woman behave like a reckless driver, then the masculine qualities of dominance – ambition, bluffing, and an inflexible insistence on one's own opinions and beliefs – can also damage her natural femininity, even though these may be the very qualities that drive her

7 M.-L. von Franz, "The Animus, the man within". In: C.G. Jung, *Man and his Symbols,* p. 189 f.

career forward. Without realizing it, women easily fall into this way of behaving, which society also expects of them if they want to be successful, for example in politics, in business, or in their roles as professionals. If they drive fast, they are applauded, but if they commit a parking offence, they are readily called a "stupid cow." The underestimation of the female cow by male consciousness in our society is obvious! However, if this happens within women themselves, as a mental process, they can only blame themselves. They are harming themselves through a wrong attitude towards their own feminine nature with which they were born. They are in imminent danger of their relatedness to others, their feminine ability to empathize, their sense of reality, their inner peace of mind, and their emotional equilibrium being undermined. This is how the woman with the two white cows in the dream can be understood.

Together, the two cows and the woman symbolize an instinctive and nurturing underpinning of both the feminine and the maternal, a kind of fundamental structure of the soul inherent in every woman. As we have seen, men, too, have a feminine aspect, which Jung called the anima. In men, the anima appears in their psyche as a female figure, while the animus appears as a male figure, or a number of male figures, in a woman's psyche.[8] We can find both animus and anima as personifications of the unconscious in films, for example, and in literature, in paintings, and of course in mythology, sagas, and fairy tales – indeed, wherever people "create images."

Nowadays, when borders between the genders seem to be blurring, this distinction between masculine and feminine, which, in depth psychology, is taken for granted, may seem affected or even antiquated. People may have different opinions about this. But when it comes to humanity in general, to the collective unconscious, male and female figures, among many others, undoubtedly do exist. They are archetypes

8 M.-L. von Franz, "The Anima, the Woman Within." In: C.G. Jung, *Man and his Symbols*: «The Anima is a personification of all psychological tendencies in a man's psyche, such as vague feelings and moods, prophetic hunches, receptiveness to the irrational, capacity for personal love, feeling for nature, and – last but not least – his relation to the unconscious.» Negatively «his anima will often express itself in irritable, depressed moods, uncertainty, insecurity and touchiness,» p. 177 f.

– structural elements of the psyche – which our efforts at equality cannot push aside. They embody the greatest opposites in the human psyche, as M.-L. von Franz once said in a private conversation. As inner images, they are as much a part of a person as one's nose or the number of one's limbs. Whether we like it or not, they also appear in our dreams, in new or old disguises. How they look, how they act, whom they are reminiscent of, and which role models in our collective memory can possibly be recognized in them, can provide us with invaluable clues about the unconscious background of our actions and thoughts. In all of this, animus and anima display characteristic differences.[9]

But for now, let's return to the cow. Let us recall the importance that the cow has had in our own and other cultures up to the present day. In Switzerland, where there is no coal, hardly any iron or any other rich raw material, the cow was, so to speak, the raw material of the alpine pastoral culture. Before corn and potatoes appeared in the 19th century and more and more food was imported, people in self-sufficient areas, though not in Central Switzerland or the lower-lying Jura region, lived mainly on livestock and some cereals. They ate dairy products at home and exported cattle and cheese.[10] The Swiss pastoral culture earned any Swiss person living abroad the less than flattering name of being a "Cow-Swiss." Even today, we export dairy products on a large scale, and they make up a substantial part of our daily diet in the form of cheese, thousands of variations of yogurt, cream products, and convenience foods. Even though we rarely demonstrate any special appreciation of the cow, it remains an important source of food. As we know, this was a different story in other cultures, where the cow was even elevated to the rank of goddess. There was not only one, but many different cow goddesses in different religions. In ancient Egypt, for example, we know of Hathor who had a human body and a cow's head with the sun disk between her horns, and the sky goddess Nut who was depicted as a cow with stars on her body. Cow goddesses

9 M.-L. von Franz, see both her articles on animus and anima in: C.G. Jung, *Man and his Symbols.*

10 A. Hauser, *Das Neue kommt. Schweizer Alltag im 19. Jahrhundert.* p. 191 f.

Fig. 2: Cows returning from a Swiss alp at the end of summer.

were Great Mother goddesses, worshipped for their maternal life-giving and food-providing qualities.[11]

Let's look at a further dream, one that concerns itself with her most important quality, namely her maternal quality. The woman who had this dream became pregnant at the age of 40 but suffered a miscarriage after her boyfriend left her. Throughout the years of depression that followed, her unconscious seemed largely to bring her anxiety, grief, restlessness,

11 For example, the Vedic cow goddess Prothivi Mata, or the Hindu sacred cow goddess Surabhi, the Germanic Audumla, the Sumerian cow goddess Ninlil or Ninsun. See. A. de Gubernatis, *Die Thiere in der indogermanischen Mythologie*. Chapter 1: "The Cow and the Bull," especially p. 37 ff. Isis also appears at times as a cow. See also: Sibylle Birkhäuser-Oeri, *Mother Figures in Fairy Tales*, p. 239.

and physical discomfort. A new period in her life then dawned in which she began to deal intensively with her dreams. One of the most important dreams of this early period was about an immobile, as if petrified, archaic mother figure in a subterranean room or cave, who looked upwards to the right, unmoving. In the years that followed, she was, in one form or another, dealing with the redemption and revitalization of this archaic mother figure, of the maternal within her psyche, that had been so brutally wounded. This was the dream:

Dream 2: The little red cow in the water.

I am in South America, on the beach. The fine sandy beach is spotlessly clean. The residents have cleared it of all trash. It's wonderful! It is a small country, probably more like an island. I move along the beach on my knees, picking up a little bit of trash here and there. This place is so beautiful, and it makes me so happy. A boat docks in the distance. It looks like a refugee boat. But they are Russians. They will have to be told the rules straight away. I see a shallow, artificial pond which looks, however, quite natural. The water is maybe 30 centimetres deep, and it is golden. A tiny red cow, like a toy cow, is walking under the water. I am surprised that she can breathe.

I would like to focus mostly on the motif of the little red cow. Firstly, however, let's look briefly at the clean beach, which the dreamer is still working on, on her knees – a devotional posture. This is perhaps an image of her long work on her dreams, whereby she was able to remove the waste material – the false, the outdated, the complex-laden material – thereby providing access to the water – to the unconscious. To maintain this access, the dream says, one must always keep an eye out for tendencies that do not want to abide by the rules, – in this instance, the Russians.

For the generation that lived through the Cold War, the Russians embodied all that was other and evil from behind the Iron Curtain. Following many years of peaceful economic and cultural exchange with the Russian giant, this view seems to be reasserting itself in the Western world today, not only in the wake of the war in Ukraine. When "the Russians" appear in a negative way in dreams, they often carry the projection of our own destructive animus opinions and aggressive prejudices, as well as a wrong and reckless kind of behaviour on the part of an unconscious shadow. Thus, they are not to be understood externally, in politics, in outer events, but rather within our own psyche.

We know only too well the workings of the human shadow that we see at every turn. Politics and society, for example, may have taken up the cause of environmental protection, but when it comes to money, power, and personal comfort, these noble principles are often quickly forgotten. According to the dream, such dishonest tendencies must be told about the rules, that is, they need to be made conscious. If not, pollution of our inner environment will take place over and over again. This is a problem that concerns us all, just as the external, worldwide pollution of the environment concerns us all. Each one of us is involved in this, for we all have our own unconscious shadow characteristics. Most of us think I'm "not like that [...]," but with our own blind egoism and unconscious desires, we can never be sure that we are not harming our inner as well as outer nature.

The image in the dream of the beach being cleaned by the people who live there seems to be the dream's way of representing the dreamer's work on this problem of "mental waste disposal" through her work on her dreams. It would seem, then, that a change in how we deal with nature could come about, not through climate programs and huge conferences, but rather through the devotion of every individual to the dream world of the unconscious. Purification and waste disposal can take place where the conscious world – the beach we know and can walk on – and the unconscious world – the unknown water – unite in a natural rhythm. This is where we can revivify our own inner, and perhaps also outer, nature and renew our entire approach to life. It seems that we all need to assume responsibility for, and take care of, our own inner mental and spiritual pollution.

Now, however, in the small pond – in the realm of the dreamer's personal unconscious – a new symbol has emerged, namely the little red cow. It is a little mother cow, so to speak, still very small and in the water, but its red colour already points to something of high emotional value. Red is the colour of blood, of lifeblood, without which we would turn into blue or green floating corpses in water. Red is also the colour of fire, of warmth, of emotion, of love. We sense that something has grown in the dreamer's psyche that has to do with the trauma she experienced around the maternal and, in the broadest sense, with her maternal unconscious, which for many years had manifested for the most part as black depression. It seems as if the fossilized mother figure in the cave or basement may be slowly coming to life. The little cow is still alive in the water, even underwater. Until now, it is only a hunch, a feeling of an instinctive, life-giving, nurturing presence in the dreamer's soul.

There are different versions of a well-known German fairy tale with the name "The Little Earth-Cow," that might give us a hint about our little red cow. Fairy tales are sometimes a great help when it comes to understanding a dream symbol, for they depict, as it were, general realities of the soul in symbolic images which we can then recognize in our dreams. This is why fairy tales occupy a place of great importance in analytical psychology, which deals with the unconscious and dreams.[12] Here is the fairy tale in brief:

The heroine of the fairy tale, Little Margaret who was to be abandoned and killed in the forest by her evil stepmother, is taken in by the "Little Earth-Cow" to live in her small house. On the condition that she will always stay with her and never betray her, the Little Earth-Cow clothes and feeds Little Margaret with milk and keeps her with her. As is usually the case in fairy tales, this promise is broken., Little Margaret reveals where she is living to her sister, who comes to the forest, whereupon the wicked stepmother has Little Earth-Cow slaughtered. Before she dies, Little Earth-Cow advises Little Margaret to go to the butcher to collect her tail, her horns, and her "Schulin" (claws), and to bury them nearby. A tree would grow there, on which, in summer and winter, apples would grow. But only Little Margaret was to pick these wonderful apples. At the end of the fairy tale, she uses them to heal the ailing son of a noble lord. Upon hearing her story, this lord takes Little Margaret, her father, and even the tree with him to his castle.[13,14]

12 See M.-L. von Franz's books *The Interpretation of Fairy Tales, Shadow and Evil in Fairytales, The Psychological Meaning of Redemption Motifs in Fairytales, Individuation in Fairytales, The Feminine in Fairy Tales, Archetypal Patterns in Fairytales, Archetypal Symbols in Fairytales.*

13 S. Birkhäuser-Oeri discusses this fairy tale in her book *Mother Figures in Fairy Tales*, p. 235–249.

14 In: A. Wesselsky, *Deutsche Märchen vor Grimm*, p. 1–10.

The Little Earth-Cow in the forest is a positive, motherly figure, reminiscent of a kind, forest fairy or helpful old woman, known to us from other fairy tales. It is a kind of nurturing, earthy nature-mother. European forests used to be large, dark, and impenetrable, a place where one could easily get lost. Countless fairy tales begin with the hero or heroine getting lost or being abandoned in the forest. We only have to think of Hansel and Gretel, or Snow White, among many others. The forest, then, in fairy tales and dreams often means a dark and threatening situation in which one cannot find one's way. But it is also a place where hermits go for introverted retreat and something new begins, where an encounter with something divine can take place. Like the mountain or the water, the forest is an image of the unconscious in which one can lose oneself, but where one can also encounter essential, new, life-bringing impulses.

The Little Earth-Cow in the forest symbolizes a hidden, helpful, natural force within a person. As an animal, this nurturing little cow embodies a motherliness that is based entirely on instinct. It is, however, a sorceress, almost a goddess, for she can die in the fairy tale and rise up again in another form. Like all divine animals in fairy tales and myths, the Little Earth-Cow represents the supremacy of instinct. As we know, the maternal instinct is a force of nature that can turn a woman into a self-sacrificing, all-embracing, warm-hearted mother who cares for everyone, or it can turn her into a smothering, constraining, or destructively overbearing mother. At the start of this fairy tale, the type of mother depicted is one who is entirely instinctive and unconscious: while she nourishes Little Margaret, she also prevents her from leaving, thereby possessively restricting and constraining her. Instinctive processes must always follow a given pattern in the same way. The Little Earth-Cow must therefore undergo change in the course of the fairy tale: in psychological language, we would say this instinctive maternal femininity in the psyche must become more conscious.

In this sense, Little Margaret's "betrayal" (by telling her sister where she is living) is a *felix culpa*, a fortunate or providential culpability, which breaks up a stagnant life situation. It had to happen, for only by it happening does the situation change, bringing renewal with it. The Earth-Cow dies and is dismembered, and Little Margaret buries it. An apple tree bearing apples that heal then grows from where it was buried. The Little

Earth-Cow has become a tree that continues to grow and bears apples that heal.

In Norse mythology, there is a goddess named *Iduna* ("the one who brings renewal," "the rejuvenator") who tends an apple tree with golden apples. She uses them to bestow eternal youth and immortality on the gods. In Christianity's creation story, the serpent seduces Eve into eating the apple from the tree of knowledge, prompting her to share it with Adam. The apple, then, is a fruit of eros, a symbol of the renewal of consciousness which Eve initiated, for after eating the apple, both Adam and Eve can distinguish good from evil and recognize themselves as man and woman. Based on these meaningful connections, we can interpret the apples that heal in this fairy tale as a more conscious, maternal-feminine kind of relatedness that is also healing for others, one that does not constrict but allows room for a woman's spiritual development.

Because of this, Little Margaret is now ready to unite with the noble lord. In psychological terms, it means that a woman is now able to connect with a masculine-spiritual/intellectual side of herself of which she was not previously aware. She is now able to acknowledge such a positive animus and realize it in her life in some way. Increasingly, she will sense when her animus is behaving poorly, upsetting herself and others, or when it is complementing her feminine nature in a positive way with a certain definiteness, independence, and intellectual open-mindedness. As in most fairy tales of this type, it seems that the goal of the nature-mother herself is to connect the feminine with this "noble lord." Finally, as a tree, she even reaches the castle.

After the happy ending of any fairy tale and all the love stories in the world, we never know how the story will continue. Can the happy union with the "noble lord" to endure? Will it be possible to keep one's trouble-making animus at bay while keeping the door open for its other aspect? These are the constant challenges in every relationship.

We know that Mother Nature has not only a helpful, healing side that always brings everything back to life, but also a terrible, cruel, dark side that has to do with death and devouring. These traits, too, are found in images of Mother Nature.

This explains all the evil stepmothers in fairy tales who want to kill the new-born child with their wily ways. They embody the dangerous aspect of the unconscious which resists becoming conscious. It constantly threatens every new developmental step a person makes through regression – a falling back into past behavioural patterns. It seems, then, that the unconscious itself has an ambivalent attitude, which is why one can never be sure where the journey is heading. Later, we will see that Hathor, the symbol of the cow goddess with the sun disk between her horns, has a special meaning in this context.

The fairy tale of the Little Earth-Cow helps us to see where the dream image of the little red cow roughly fits in. The little red cow in the water is the equivalent of the Little Earth-Cow in the forest. In this, we recognize the archetypal – i.e., common to all humanity – initial stage of a development in the dreamer's psyche, a development that could lead to a profound transformation of the maternal-feminine within. This could mean one feels less depressed and insecure, and more self-confident, calm, and contemplative in this more feminine way of relating to and assessing other people. And perhaps it also means harmonizing one's intellectual strivings with one's own feminine nature, thereby replacing a disturbing animus with respectful, mutual relatedness. The wedding, which always comes at the end of this type of fairy tale, is the archetypal image of the union of the male and female opposites within one personality. Out of this, a child can be born: a new development can begin. The dream of the little red cow is an encouraging, supportive sign of life from the unconscious psyche of the woman who dreamed it.

One might easily think that fairy tales or dreams that feature a mother and a heroine are simply about women, but that is not the case. Every mother shapes her son's relationship to women and to the feminine, particularly to his anima. Furthermore, it is not only in women that the problem of the maternal – or, as we say in depth psychology, the mother complex – is concerned with giving birth to something new, to greater consciousness: this is also true for men. A man's 'birthing process,' his creative process, is closely connected with his relationship to his mother, to the maternal unconscious. Men can also have birth dreams!

Fairy tales show us how important it is for the hero or heroine to behave in the right way when they encounter wisdom, the spirit of the unconscious – the old man in the forest, the dwarf, the unknown companion, and so on. For without their help, the hero or heroine will not be able to reach their goal, lift the treasure, overcome the evil wizard or witch, or win the princess or prince. Sometimes this help comes in the form of a Little Earth-Cow, an entirely maternal, feminine, and even animal-like figure. But she seems to want to reach the same goal as the old man in the forest. Spirit and nature, then, are, in a sense, aspects of the same thing in the unconscious. Dreams sometimes emphasize the natural aspect (e.g. the cow), while at other times more the spiritual aspect (e.g. the old man in the wood).

One can embrace such a hint from a dream by thinking about it, questioning it, carrying it around and incubating it, even ruminating on it like a cow, or one can shelve it as incomprehensible, in the same way some arrogant fairy tale characters do when they disparage or even insult the helpful old man or woman. In fairy tales, as in the spiritual realm, this usually has nasty consequences. Some piece of nourishing food then lies undigested in our stomachs – an unhealthy condition, that in the long run, can make the whole organism ill.

The next dream is about the birth of something new. The woman who had this dream was pregnant at the time she dreamt it. The dream presents us with a completely different image, far-removed from the motif of the Little Earth-Cow. But here, too, the fairy tale will be helpful in understanding the dream.

Dream 3: The cow that gave birth

I am in a meadow where there are cows, very large, imposing cows, light beige-white pied. One of these cows lies down on her back and bends her hind legs, like a woman giving birth. She even propped herself up a little on the elbows of her front legs. Spellbound, I stare at what is happening. I sit down in the meadow and from where I am sitting, I have a crystal-clear view of a gigantic cavity opening between her legs. She pushes something out of this huge cavity. I can see more and more of it. Is it a calf that is being pushed out? At first, I think it is, and this is what I am expecting. But instead, it is a small human being, very compact, like a little Buddha. It is a baby, but at the same time, it looks like the little statue of a wise person meditating. I can hardly believe what I am seeing.

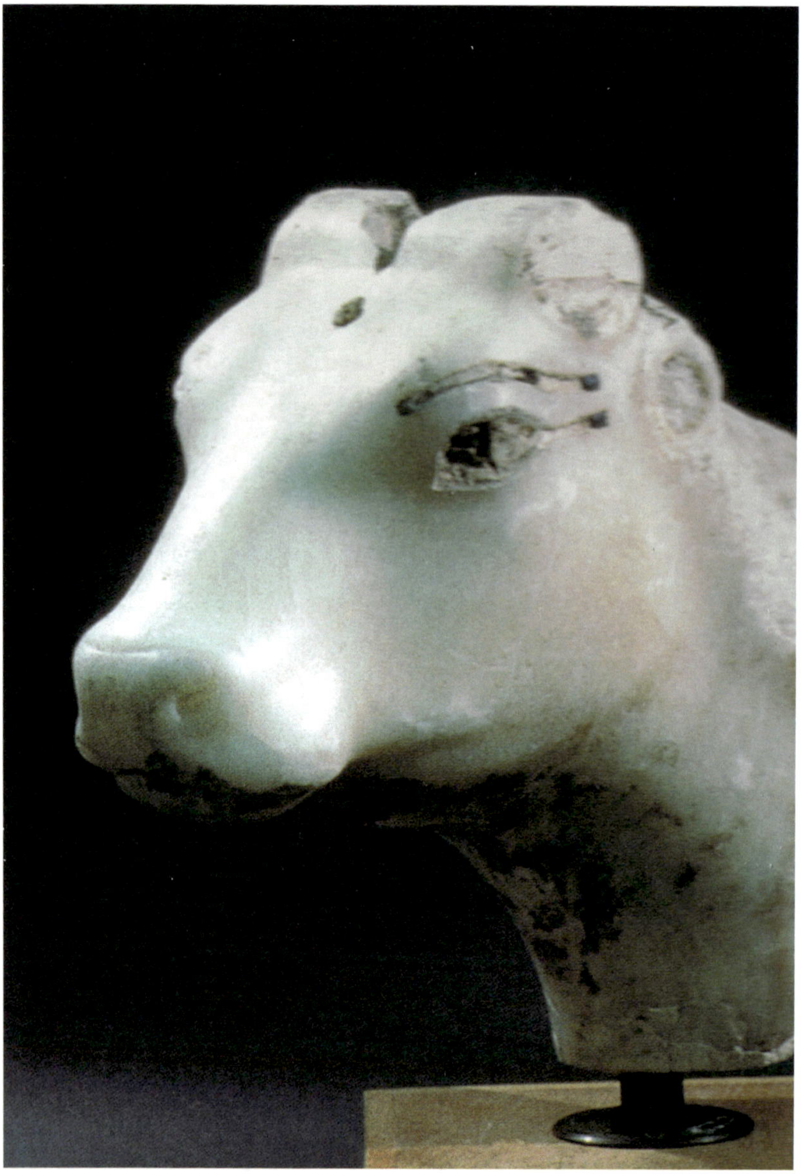

Fig. 3: Head of the cult statue of the goddess Hathor. Burial temple of Hatschepsut, 1465 B.C., London, British Museum.

As in the fairy tale of the Little Earth-Cow, this is also about a possible transformation, a new birth, within the psyche of a dreamer. This, too, is no ordinary cow. She is huge, and out of her mighty, cavernous womb she gives birth not to a calf, but to a human figure. Caves are associated with the mother goddesses. Such caves were places of worship and were understood exactly as the dream depicts, namely as a maternal womb and birthing cave. Caves were where the gods were born, for example the seat of Eileithya, a pre-Greek goddess of childbirth in Crete, or the birth caves of the fertility goddess Demeter in Sicily.

We can say, then, that the dreamer is not witnessing a profane birth, but a divine one. In an extensive collection of dreams of pregnant women made in the 1990's, the theme of a divine or superhuman birth occurs so frequently one might readily infer it has a special meaning.[15] In such dreams, one can often recognize the maturation of an inner process unfolding. But these dreams also place the birth of a child within the greater context of a universal creative act on the part of human nature in general. Because this act of creation manifests all over the world in similar symbols, it also describes a universal human process that can unfold in each one of us. Something new, something unexpected, a new world view, a new attitude, a new idea, a new way of approaching, inventing, creating things, etc., can suddenly rise up from the unconscious. Throughout the history of humankind, divine births have occurred throughout all the ages and in all cultures. The birth of Christ, which, at that time, equated to the birth of a completely new understanding of the world, was just such an extraordinary event. In its wake, Christianity spread like wildfire throughout the Mediterranean region and fundamentally changed the world of that time.

So, what are we to make of this dream of the cow giving birth? This act of creation produces a human child, a baby, but one that looks like a little Buddha, or like the small statue of a wise person meditating. What do these figures mean, and why are they born from an animal, from a cow?

The cow as a mother who brings forth a human being falls, as it were, somewhere between the animal and the human. In this, she is reminiscent of many goddesses and gods who were represented with a

15 See R. Abt, I. Bosch, V. Mackrell, *Dream Child.*

human body and an animal head, or the reverse. Not least among them is the ancient Egyptian cow goddess Hathor with a human body and a cow's head, bearing a sun disk between her horns. What were the people who created such symbolic human-animal or animal-human images trying to express? What was so important to them that they even worshipped these images as religious symbols? And what does it mean when a symbol like this appears in the dream of a modern person?

It would undoubtedly be wrong to think 'animal' here refers to any real animal. In all cultures, and in our fairy tales, there are innumerable stories of animals who act and speak as if they were human. "The donkey said to the dog, 'Come with me to Bremen [...],'" and so on. From the standpoint of depth psychology, these animals are symbolic representations of animalistic, instinctive human behaviour. When we react instinctively, we do so spontaneously, reflexively, without any thought. We leap, realizing only afterwards that we have avoided a danger. We perform countless instinctive actions every day, without any conscious intention. A 'god-animal' that appears to be partially human indicates that such animalistic, instinctive behaviours point to a process of becoming more conscious of their specifically human quality, as M.-L. von Franz explains.[16] This was clearly the case in the culture of ancient Egyptian and wherever there were animal-human gods and goddesses. Because she brings forth a human child, the cow of our dream can also be understood as an animal-human hybrid.

From a depth psychological point of view, we can say that animalistic, instinctive behaviours belong to those layers of the human psyche that are most deeply unconscious – the maternal, primordial foundation of the psyche, out of which all consciousness evolves. C.G. Jung writes rather poetically that these deepest, unconscious layers represent «the immemorial world of archetypal possibilities, where [...] slumbers the 'divine child,' patiently awaiting his conscious realization.»[17] From the nature of its birth, we may conclude that this dream-cow's child is just such a divine child. Mythological, divine children always have both a special significance and destiny. This is confirmed not only in our fairy tales, but in myths and mythological stories told the world over, and at all times.

16 M.-L. von Franz, *Archetypal Dimensions of the Soul,* p. 111.

17 C.G. Jung, *Symbols of Transformation,* [CW 5], § 508.

Fig. 4: Cow goddess Hathor. Saqqara, 600–500 B.C., Cairo.

On a more intimate, personal level, the child in dreams primarily symbolizes something new that is still undeveloped, sometimes childish, or simply of the future, something which can grow and become conscious in a person.[18] But the dream also says that the newborn child is no ordinary child: it is like a little Buddha, or like a statuette of a meditating sage. If we look to India or any other Buddhist country, the Buddha or wise yogi is worshipped as a holy or saintly figure who has acquired higher wisdom and awareness through meditation. In religious tradition, the Indian god Shiva, like Buddha or Christ, is a messenger of divine will. All three are superior spirits in contact with the divine. Like the infant Jesus or baby Moses, Buddha, Christ, and many other semi-divine heroes of mythology were, as it turns out, divine from the outset. Such a child therefore symbolizes not only 'the new,' emerging out of the unconscious, but also 'the old,' the superior spirit, a bearer of ancient knowledge, which, from time immemorial, has always existed as a possibility in the unconscious and comes to life in this child. These children are, therefore, simultaneously young and old, which is why the little Buddha in the dream is both child and aged meditator.

How does this relate to the dreamer? On the one hand, this extraordinary birth can be seen as the spontaneous emergence of an undeveloped aspect of this woman's individuality – the child. The symbol of the old sage, on the other hand, seems to point to some future spiritual potential within her.

The general message of the dream hints at a spontaneous renewal within her feminine nature, or, seen more broadly, as the emergence of a spiritual principle out of the maternal, primordial foundation of her psyche. This is not an easy thing to simply accept. How does something like this unfold without our input and knowledge?

Some people are startled when they realize for the first time that the unconscious can act autonomously. They are afraid of losing control, which may indeed occur. They feel as if they are about to lose their grip on the reins of the horses that have been pulling their wagon up until then.

18 M.-L. von Franz, *The Interpretation of Fairy Tales*, p. 52: «That is why it is also a symbol of the self, the possible inner, future wholeness that is inherent in the unconscious psyche of all human beings. The self, according to our definition, is the centre of the self-regulating system of the psyche, on which the welfare of the individual depends.»

We are accustomed to setting our own course, to attributing the invention of something new to our own intellect, reasoning, or urge to explore, etc. There is nothing wrong with this if we act with and not against the unconscious. But how can we be sure we are in accordance with it? The first step would probably be to accept that we cannot be in control of everything. As the dream describes, the spirit, or spiritual principle, can autonomously emerge from the unconscious realm of natural instincts and drives at any time. This is especially true for a woman in pregnancy where seemingly everything has to do with pure nature and nothing with spirit, for a birth is probably the most extreme experience of being at the mercy of nature.

In the dream, however, the little Buddha is still a child, a baby even, and the figure of the wise meditator initially looks like a small, lifeless statuette. The dreamer, then, needs to focus on, experience, vivify, and let grow what is emerging as 'spiritual' from within. This includes patiently paying attention to what emerges from the unconscious in the form of dreams. It is as if she had to care for and nurture, swaddle, and nourish a newborn baby to help it grow into life.

In our Western culture, many people are fascinated by Eastern religions like Buddhism, Hinduism, Taoism, etc. The dreamer, too, meditated and performed rituals from the introverted world of the East. According to Jung, however, Eastern and Western points of view are like fire and water and they cannot be mixed. «Instead of learning the spiritual techniques of the East by heart and imitating them in a thoroughly Christian way, […] with a corresponding forced attitude, it would be far more to the point to find out whether there exists in the unconscious an introverted tendency similar to that which has become the guiding spiritual principle of the East. […] It seems to me that we have really learned something from the East when we understand that the psyche contains riches enough without having to be primed from outside. […] We must get at the Eastern values from within and not from without, seeking them in ourselves, in the unconscious.»[19]

19 C.G. Jung, "Eastern Religion." In: *Psychology and Religion: West and East* [CW 11], p. 481 f.

This is what the dream of a cow – the sacred animal of the Hindus – giving birth to Buddha seems to express. Rather than being born through the simple imitation of Eastern spiritual practices, the introverted wisdom of the East is born from within one's own psyche. This would be the birth of the little Buddha, the wise meditator, from the cow. As I mentioned earlier, the pregnant woman who had this dream was living at the time in an atmosphere of incense and Eastern rituals, of meditation and spiritual search. The dream seems to replace this attitude with a more 'Western' psychological standpoint, one that encompasses an 'Eastern,' more introverted conception of the divine through the figures of the Buddha and the meditating sage.

As experience shows, dreams seem to have a secret knowledge about our potentialities, both past and future, about deeper connections in our personal lives and in the world at large. Such "knowledge,' arising from the seemingly purely instinctive realm of the unconscious, influences our thinking, our ideas, our attitudes, and our actions. This does not take the form of rational decisions, derived from the prevailing external circumstances of our life; rather, it is a kind of inner perception that has to do with feeling, with 'smelling', as it were, with ideas, thoughts, and intuitions and often a feeling that something makes sense or not. We give birth to these perceptions, to this hitherto unconscious 'knowledge,' by bringing them into the realm of conscious cognition, i.e., by becoming conscious of unconscious, spiritual contents.

Our dream of the supernatural cow-birth seems to complement the unfolding of the purely natural process of pregnancy and birth with an expanded view – an expanded spiritual horizon – that can grow out of the maternal unconscious in the same way a child does.

Here I would like to mention a short but astonishing dream that was had by another woman. *She dreamed that a man and a woman brought her a wonderful black and white cow that had a golden ball between its mighty horns*,[20] an astonishing image given that it corresponds quite precisely to

20 Dream of an African woman: *I am asleep in my grandfather's kraal again. Something wakes me and I notice a white light outside the entryway. Two men and a woman enter. The woman leads in a cow. The cow is magnificent, black and white, and on her head, between her huge crescent shaped horns, is a golden ball.*

Fig. 5: Worship of the cow goddess. Sarcophagus of Khonsu. 1295–1186.

the image of the ancient Egyptian goddess Hathor/Isis, who carries a sun disk between her horns. Why this woman, who was not from Egypt and had probably never heard of the cow goddess Hathor/Isis, dreamed of this image, we do not know. We do know, however, that the Hathor cow corresponds to an archetype of the maternal-feminine in the unconscious, collective psyche. Such an archetype can manifest anywhere in the world in all the things that people dream of, invent, conceive of, fantasize about, or create in some form. The mother image of an Inuit tribe will differ from that of indigenous South Americans, just as the mother image of Aboriginal and Torres Strait Islander people will differ from that of the African San. But beyond these cultural differences, the common, fundamental aspect of the archetype can be recognized everywhere. This archetypal image of Hathor, here with the sun disk, can perhaps help us to better understand the dream of the cow birth.

With the sun disk on her head, the Hathor cow differs from other cow goddesses, for example from Isis/Nut, the heavenly cow with stars in her womb. In one myth, Hathor is described as a creator goddess who carries the sun-god Re in her womb to whom she gives birth every morning. The connection of the divine cow with the sun therefore has a particular meaning.[21]

Sunlight is the prerequisite for being able to see and recognize things at all. The sun is therefore the fitting and comprehensive image for the cognizant light of consciousness, which is not to be confused with intellect. 'To throw light on something' means in our colloquial language to make something clear – to become conscious of it. As most living organisms would perish in constant darkness, the sun equates to life for humans, animals and plants. Without it, we would all freeze to death. Therefore, from a mythological point of view, it makes sense that the sun symbolizes the warming, nurturing, maternal aspect of nature. Hathor's solar disc can thus be seen as a light of consciousness arising from the most ancient layers of the human soul. As with the Buddha-child of the above dream, we are not talking about our purposeful, rational, conscious intellect. Rather, we are talking about the possibility of consciousness that comes from the "instinctive-archaic foundation of our thinking,"[22] which shines forth in dreams, in unconscious imaginative activity, in everything that unconsciously moves us at any given moment or motivates us and causes us to act and imagine in surprising or incomprehensible ways.

As Marie-Louise von Franz explains, we can recognize this spirit or light from the most ancient layers of the unconscious psyche as that intrinsically unknown element in nature which creates meaningful order.[23] This would be a light of nature – the sun between the horns of Hathor. Nature is not simply chaotic. The natural, instinctive processes of animal behaviour, for example, are typical for every species and cannot simply be changed. We humans, too, cannot arbitrarily violate certain 'species-specific' conditions. In the same way that physical symptoms alert us to poor eating habits, for example, or nightmares indicate a mental problem, so, too, does our inner compass swing into action when we set off in the

21 See A. de Gubernatis, *Die Thiere in der indogermanischen Mythologie,* in which he presents a wealth of mythological material connecting the cow to the sun.

22 C.G. Jung, *Symbols of Transformation,* [CW 5], § 38.

23 See M.-Louise von Franz, *The Psychological Meaning of Redemption Motifs in Fairytales,* p.49.

wrong direction. Thus, there must be, according to Marie-Louise von Franz, an unknown regulating factor within us that is at the service of life.[24] It reacts to any one-sidedness in our attitude and behaviour with mental or physical illness.

We can assume that this unknown, life-enhancing factor which we call spirit is what the meditator or Buddha of the previous dream experiences in his immersion. All philosophies and religious systems use an infinite number of images to describe it in their own way. Referencing the Indian concept of the *Atman*, C. G. Jung named this central archetype "the Self,"[25] and he went on to prove its existence with innumerable examples of concepts from the history of ideas, and not least with examples from the dreams and fantasies of his patients. Of all the symbolic images with which man has tried to describe this invisible, ordering, and illuminating spirit, the sun is an essential one. The great simplicity of the cow goddess Hathor with her sun disk makes it a compelling symbol of the origin of the spirit arising from within – a still valid, intuitive symbol of the self. In the *I Ching*, an ancient Chinese book of oracles,[26] which C. G. Jung studied in detail, Hexagram 30 says, «The cow is the symbol of extreme docility. By cultivating in himself an attitude of compliance and voluntary dependence, man acquires clarity without sharpness and finds his place in the world.»[27]

Dream 4: The statue of Hathor in the Museum of Ancient History

I hear that we are planning an excursion to the Museum of Ancient History with a group of colleagues. I tell a colleague that I am already very familiar with it and that I therefore find the decision rather unfortunate. A little later I am with this woman in the museum (underground room) and

24 Ibid., p. 53.

25 C. G. Jung, *Letters*, Vol. I, 1906–1950, Letter from 7.09.1945, p. 359. Jung writes there: «This nomenclature is no invention of mine. It existed with the same meaning for the same thing for hundreds of years before I did.»

26 R. Wilhelm (ed.), *I Ching or Book of Changes*.

27 C. G. Jung, "Foreword to the 'I Ching'." In: *Psychology and Religion: West and East*, [CW 11], § 964–1117.

it looks quite different to what I know. It is larger and filled with many large figures and statues. We are alone in here. I go to a Hathor statue in cow form which I find particularly moving and brilliant (it seems I already know it). An elegant cow in mid-stride in a golden glow, it comes up to my waist. I point it out to the other woman, hug the statue around the neck and feel very pleased.

Why does a mother image from ancient Egypt appear in the dream of a modern Western woman? Why has the archetype of the maternal-feminine chosen to express itself in this way? After all, it could also have used a symbolic image from our Nordic, Western culture. What happened to a mother-image such as this one, and did it ever exist? Perhaps the Virgin Mary of Christianity is a mother-image, though she lacks the earthy, dark, instinctive traits, and can therefore only cover a part of the feminine. We must, then, reach farther back to the wise women and shamans of the pre-Christian, European forest-dwelling peoples, who were of great importance to their tribe. They were rich in their knowledge of nature, which, as healers, they used, also when attending a birth. The Christian missionaries viewed the natural powers these women had as 'superstition' and did all they could to dispel it. They were accused of being witches and of being in league with the devil, which is why there are still so many witches in our fairy tales. Only in the form of inconspicuous little mothers and helpful old women who protect the hero and heroine from the man-eater or robber and act as a guide can these positive, wise women still be found in these tales.

Within our Western, Christian culture, it is only in fairy tales that we still have a generally accepted, religiously classified image of the nature-mother archetype with all its positive and negative aspects. The witch aspect must also be a part of it! Jung summarizes the essential features of the mother archetype thus:

«The qualities associated with it are maternal solicitude and sympathy; the magic authority of the female; the wisdom and spiritual exaltation that transcend reason; any helpful instinct or impulse; all that is benign, all that cherishes and sustains, that fosters growth and fertility. The place of magic transformation and rebirth, together with the underworld and its inhabitants, are presided over by the mother. On the negative side

Fig. 6: Hathor cow in tomb of Seti I, Egypt. Aquarelle made by R. Hay after 1824.

the mother archetype may connote anything secret, hidden, dark; the abyss, the world of the dead, anything that devours, seduces, and poisons, that is terrifying and inescapable like fate.»[28]

Jung described and documented these characteristics of the mother archetype in detail in, among others, his work *Symbols of Transformation*.

As one can see from this all too short enumeration, the 'mother' is a structural disposition common to all people. It forms, as it were, the matrix of all human beings, of both the female and male psyche. In our Christian culture, she leads a shadowy existence. The lack of «the characteristic relation of the mother-image to the earth, darkness, the abysmal side of the bodily man with his animal passions and instinctual nature, and to 'matter' in general,»[29] as Jung says, has serious consequences for every woman

28 C. G. Jung, *The Archetypes and the Collective Unconscious,* [CW 9/I], § 158.

29 Ibid., § 195.

and for the general concept of the feminine. This one-sidedly positive Christian image of the feminine makes demands on women which, to this day, they can seldom fulfil, no matter how hard they try. We still adhere to the ancient ideal of beauty and the romantic requirement for a woman to have a loving, sociable, cheerful, and self-sacrificing character. Beautiful, extraverted, self-confident, seductive women dazzle on the Internet as role models, putting young girls and many other women under desperate pressure to succeed.

The fact that women are and can be much more than that is part of the forgotten shadow aspect of a woman's nature. It comes as no surprise, then, that when these shadow aspects suddenly and violently erupt, it is very difficult for women and men to deal with them. Passionate jealousy, for example, which of course should never exist, is one of the most common problems destroying relationships and leading people to seek help. And not only for women! A man's relationship to the archetype of the maternal-feminine, however, is essentially different from that of a woman's, but that is another story!

If a woman is unable to feel and accept herself in her natural wholeness, with all the positive and negative aspects of the archetype of the feminine, she readily loses her bearings with an animus way of thinking that is unhealthy for her; it is a masculine, rational mode of thought that generates unpleasant consequences. The spirit of the unconscious becomes a rigid, know-it-all, and her feminine feeling, instinct, and common sense is suppressed. This dynamic disrupts relationships and ultimately makes women unhappy in themselves.

Perhaps it is this loss of relationship to the mother archetype, to these fundamental properties of the unconscious psyche, that has led today's ethnologists and ethnobiologists to try to revive ancient rituals.[30] They fill seminars, lecture halls, and experiential events talking about them, and they sell a lot of books. For some, it seems to be their own affinity with nature that forces them to realize how we, both women and men, suffer from a lack of nature's healing wisdom today.

30 See contributions of W.-D. Storl in ethnobotany and ethnomedicine, as example of his many books: *Unsere 5 heiligen Bäume, Weitblicke, Wir sind Geschöpfe des Waldes.*

Just how far this can lead an audience or readership to adopt a more conscious approach to the spiritual forces that are the source of all these natural rituals and of their belief in nature spirits, I am not sure. In view of the psychological problems facing modern society today, a more conscious approach would certainly be urgently needed.[31] Perhaps some people are able to access the spiritual reality behind our rationalized and mechanized modern world simply through meditative contemplation of plants, trees, and stones. After all, the purpose of a nature ritual would be to connect with nature, with the natural and healing forces of the soul. It is probably no coincidence that it is mainly women who respond to this kind of archaic access to one's own inner nature. The increasing popularity of medicinal and edible plants and herbs, ancient preservation methods, organic nutrition, and animal welfare issues is in keeping with this.

We have understood that the image of the cow goddess Hathor / Isis embodies a symbolic image of the 'mother' in dreams. This spiritual reality finds only partial representation in our Christian culture, for example in ancient Norse cultural relics and fairy tales. But in the highly developed culture and mythology of ancient Egypt, the 'mother' was greatly revered in the mythological figure of Hathor. As a goddess, Hathor embodies a supreme value, a cosmic, maternal principle, and a feminine principle of fertility and renewal.

One can ask why such an image should still be important for us today. Is it not more meaningful to fight for equal rights for women and for the concerns of feminism? Without neglecting these external aspects, it nevertheless makes sense to look inward at the symbol of the cow. Only if our efforts for greater female empowerment and independence are carried from within, for example by an instinctive calmness

31 M.-L. von Franz, *Interpretation of Fairy Tales*, p. 9: «Another modern movement consists of a group of ethnologists, archeologists, and specialists in mythology and the comparative history of religion, practically all of whom know Jung and Jungian psychology but try to interpret mythological motifs omitting Jung's hypotheses – and naturally the name of Jung as well – and to make indirect use of Jung's discoveries. They write books with titles such as *The Great Goddess* or *The Threefold* Godhead or *The Hero*, and they do not take as a starting point the human individual and his psychic structure, which has produced these symbols, but they sit in the middle of the archetype, so to speak, and let it amplify itself, poetically and 'scientifically.'»

and a natural, nurturing eros, will they not result in more fruitless gender struggles and in providing the animus with more room to interfere.

As we mentioned earlier, the archetype of the feminine contains not only the positive and the nurturing, but also the passionate, the possessive, the devouring – all the terrible aspects of nature itself. Our awareness, then, must include not only the good, but also these dangerous aspects of the 'inner' feminine. Any uncritical valorization of women that establishes 'women quotas' in the professional and political realm therefore misses this spiritual reality, often bringing unexpected and unpleasant consequences with it.

The sun disk adds an additional symbol to the purely maternal-feminine nature of the cow goddess. According to our earlier interpretation, it is a symbol of the unknown, life-promoting factor we call spirit. To the Egyptians, the sun was the guarantor of all order, and the source of supreme awareness.[32] Thus, the Egyptian Hathor cow and its sun disk also conveys the idea that rather than being mutually exclusive, a woman's life honestly lived goes hand in hand with spiritual clarity.

The golden statue of Hathor in the subterranean room of the Museum of Ancient History indicates a relationship that is still more imagined than lived to this precious feminine-spiritual value. She is not to be found in the place where the dreamer thinks she knows her way around – an important detail of the dream, for which, at this point, there is presumably a personal reason. The statue is still hidden and somewhat 'off to the side,' but the dreamer has a warm feeling about it, an intimate familiarity with it, as if it were already known to her. We cannot go into the personal situation of this intelligent and multi-talented woman here. We can say, however, that it can be particularly difficult, especially in such psychological circumstances, to do justice to the various, often contradictory, demands of one's own inner nature. Often, however, particularly profound creative processes emerge out of difficult outer and inner conditions. At bottom, the golden Hathor statue signifies both the secret nature and source of the creative, feminine inner life.

The next dream was had by a middle-aged female artist:

32 M.-L. von Franz, *On Dreams and Death,* p. 66.

Fig. 7: Golden pendant. Isis/Hathor, 1069–945 B.C., Egyptian Museum Cairo.

Dream 5: The ox-child

I am walking through the hall of a music academy, towards a large glass door that leads into a park. On my right is the reception desk, and my path crosses that of a strange child who is walking towards this reception desk, having just won a prize for being a musical genius. The boy is about 6 years old and quite short, and he is wearing a hood. As we meet in the middle, I see his face which is a mix of both a human face and that of an ox. He is very aware of how unusual he is, and his expression conveys a tremendous, pent-up tension. I am deeply touched by this chance meeting, but I continue toward the door.

In the next scene, this child is walking up a wide, public staircase that connects a park from a lower street to an upper main street with wide sidewalks. The boy walks between a man on his left and this man's teenage son on his right. The man is holding some papers (a file) in front of the strange, hooded child to hide his facial features from the people. I was about to climb the stairs when I crossed their path. Again, I was deeply touched by that strange and tense face.

I am now in the park, on its lower level. I am sitting on a wooden bench, and I am holding the ox-child in my arms. The boy is much younger now, and I calm him by holding him against my chest. His hair is strange. It is curly, and at the base of his skull it has an inverted triangle that looks like pubic hair. A surprising smell emanates from it, a mixture of ozone and sulphur – my thought in the dream – which is not unpleasant, just strange. A woman is sitting at the other end of the bench with her son. She looks at the child curiously, but upon seeing the triangle, she complains to me that the child is creepy. I stare at her intensely until she looks away.

In the last scene, I'm back on the upper street, surrounded by people walking by. The boy is a little older again, about 6 years old, and he is walking away. I watch him disappear into the crowd with mixed feelings of tenderness and acceptance. In my arms he had been able to completely relax; he even fell asleep for a moment. I know that this interlude helped him to release pressure, to let go of some of the tension for a moment, and that was really the only thing I could do for him.

Who is this boy with the face of an ox? This mysterious figure can instantly be recognized as the child of the archetypal cow-mother, as we have come to know her. His facial features are surprising, mysterious, and difficult to comprehend. The only thing that one can be sure of is that he must come from another world, and his appearance is as surprising as his disappearance.

Initially, he appears as a musical genius, a child prodigy who has won a music competition. Music is something mysterious, even if today it can be heard in every form from every loudspeaker. It can thrill or inspire us to dance ecstatically; it can move us to tears, put us in high spirits, or evoke melancholy mournfulness. We listen to music, for example, at a funeral, when we want to be silent and give space to our feelings. We have no reasonable explanation of who or what brings about this connection between music and our emotions. Music is a cultural achievement of mysterious origin: for archaic man, it progressed out of natural sounds – such as birdsong, wind and the sound of waves – and rhythms which archaic humans used to channel their imagination, their feelings, and their state of mind into dance and expressive movement. Music has always been used to transport unconscious emotion onto a higher creative level. The ability to create music and culture was usually attributed to the gods. Today, we can simply say that music in its original sense has something to do with the soul.

As a musical genius, the ox-child in the dream is symbolically closely related to a creative force of nature, one that gives rise to music in a person. It is, so to speak, the unconscious itself that stimulates music. Using instruments or one's own voice, it prompts a person to consciously express unconscious moods, feelings, or inner images, to compose music, to write it down in notes, and to pass it on. From further symbolism of the ox-boy we will see that he himself embodies this creative force of nature.

Perhaps the beginning of this dream underscores the emotion and intense feeling on the part of the dreamer that the encounter with this mysterious, unknown figure initially triggers. Normally, when we wake up with such a dream image, even if we are touched or frightened, it seems so far away, and we usually cannot do much with it. We are neither able nor willing to pursue it, to think about it, to lovingly carry it around with us, and to brood upon it. Even though the dreamer is deeply impressed, she nevertheless continues on her way, and this could well have been the end of the dream.

Instead, there is a second and a third scene which leads into the fourth and final scene. This number symbolism is not accidental. We find it in countless fairy tales: three tasks, three attempts, three events, and finally the solution. The number three has to do with movement and time, the inexorable flow of past, present, and future.[33] Goddesses of fate, such as the three Germanic Norns, are associated with the passing of time and of a life unfolding. The symbolism of the numbers three and four in how the dream unfolds indicate a dynamic event now constellating in the dreamer's inner life. Something from the unconscious is drawing attention to itself, apparently wanting to become visible. Thus, the number three can indicate a process of change unfolding within the psyche. Something is beginning to shift. As we will see, the number three in dreams is meaningful in other ways, too.

In their first encounter, the dreamer momentarily notices only that the boy is wearing a hood, and that his face has a strange mix of both human and oxen features. She also senses the tremendous tension from which the child seems to suffer.

The hood, which hides the true ancestry of the child, already gives us a hint of his otherworldly origins. It is reminiscent of the dwarves and brownies of our legends and fairy tales that originally descended from the chthonic gods of Greek antiquity, the dactyls (finger- or thumblings). Though inconspicuous and often misshapen, they were believed to have powerful miraculous powers, and they wear a special, pointed head covering (pileus), which is their secret sign of recognition. Traditionally, the dactyls were believed to be the teachers of Orpheus who invented musical rhythm.[34] Thus, we have the relationship of the hooded child to music. Mysterious dwarf gods and brownies have to do with creative energy from the unconscious. It is through music – through feeling – that this nature-like creativity can transmit unconscious content into consciousness.

The first encounter with the hooded child, who clearly comes from another world, is, psychologically speaking, an initial, intuitive feeling or

33 M.-L. von Franz, *The Interpretation of Fairy Tales,* p. 89 f. See also: C. G. Jung, *Psychology and Religion: West and East,* [CW 11].

34 C. G. Jung, *Psychology and Alchemy,* [CW 12], § 180, 183.

Fig. 8: Germanic-Nordic God. Bronze statuette. Reykjavik, National Museum, Hamlyn archives.

fantasy which the dreamer does not pursue. Such an image emerging from the unconscious is so alien to the conscious world that it seems impossible to make contact with it. It disappears again.

Why, we wonder repeatedly, is it so difficult to understand the symbolic images of the unconscious, to understand dreams? If the unconscious clearly wants to get something across, why does it disguise it and make it disappear again, like the carrot before the donkey? Are we doing something wrong? Or better: Is there something we should be doing?

Jung has shown that through their experiments, the ancient alchemists were seeking to understand the mystery of matter. They focused entirely on their thoughts and fantasies which they tried to express through symbolic images. Nowadays, we would say that they focused on unconscious, mental processes which revealed themselves through the transformation and transmutation of substances in their experiments. Similarly, for people today, it is a matter of focusing on creative, transformative, and developmental processes within the psyche which the unconscious often independently sets in motion.[35] In a nutshell, then, this is apparently what we can do.

When dreams, moods, inner and outer difficult situations and events trouble us, we can often do nothing but expose ourselves to the impulses of the unconscious without running away. Most often, we are not ready to do this until we have no other choice. However, as Jung points out, this approach to the unconscious often creates an almost unbearable tension, for unconscious processes and conscious life are often incompatible.[36] The tension and suffering in the face of the child are an indication of the suffering not only in consciousness, but also in the unconscious.

Experience and dreams confirm that along with transporting new impulses into consciousness, the unconscious also swallows them up again. Dreams that we desperately want to remember, disappear the moment we begin to recall them or want to write them down; important insights once delivered fade away, never to be found again; memories appear and disappear before we can recall them. The unconscious seems

35 C.G. Jung, *Psychology and Alchemy,* [CW 12], §43, illustration 3 shows an inverted triangle, like the one on the child's head in the dream.

36 C.G. Jung, *Symbols of Transformation,* [CW 5], § 186.

both to want and to not want to move toward consciousness. It wants us to become conscious of something that could expand our personality with some previously unknown or misunderstood aspect, and yet, again and again, everything seems to slip away. We must endure this, even when we seem to have no connection to the unconscious, when we have no dreams for a long time, or only dreams that seem to give no answer to the most pressing current questions.

Thus, for the moment, the dreamer once again loses sight of the strange, hooded child, until, apparently by chance, she encounters him again. Accompanied by a man and his son, the child climbs an open staircase from a lower level in a park. Higher up, there are roads, traffic, sidewalks, etc. It is the level of the mechanized, urban world, where one can move along predetermined paths. This is the level of the mind and intellect, of an organized consciousness. As the dreamer prepares to descend the stairs, her path crosses that of the ox-child and his companions. In the third scene, she finds herself down in the park. This is a natural, green environment where people can relax, where one can be alone with one's thoughts and feelings. The park is a more natural environment than the upper street, but it is still an environment created by humans. Perhaps it represents an ideal area between consciousness and the unconscious, a place where both sides can approach each other.

So now we are dealing with the different levels on which an unconscious content can appear. The second encounter with the ox-child takes place on the second level, on the large and open staircase straddling both levels; the third encounter takes place on the third level, down in the park. What special significance could the stairs have that connect the different levels? Steps and ladders play a special role in alchemy. Jung explains they indicate, as it were, a step-by-step process of transformation taking place within the soul.[37] This explains why spiritual development via Internet programs, or all the many quick and successful fixes that are on offer, does not work. Although these quick successes are real, they are often based on suggestion, which means their success fades after a

37 C.G. Jung, *Psychology and Alchemy,* [CW 12], § 68, fig. 15: The *scala lapidis*, representing the stages of the alchemical process. And: E. F. Edinger, *Anatomy of the Psyche,* p. 135–139.

shorter or longer period. The unconscious has its own rhythm; while we can support it, we cannot willfully accelerate it.

The ascension of the child and his companions can be seen as the ascension of this mysterious content towards the level of consciousness. The dreamer, on the other hand, moves toward the lower level of the park, that is, toward a natural relationship with the unconscious. Two tendencies meet on the middle flight of stairs: one is the tendency of the unconscious to move 'up,' to approach consciousness as an intuition, dream image, or fantasy; the other is that of consciousness moving downward, to confront an unusual feeling or fantasy from the unconscious, even to notice it at all. The subtle detail of their 'crossing' can be taken as a subtle hint of having to bear the 'cross' that such an encounter with the incomprehensible, unconscious images can mean!

In the child's two companions, the dreamer recognizes the threefold nature of the new content for the first time. Father and son are, so to speak, a part of the hooded child. As mentioned earlier, we see such a connection in many threefold (triadic) mythological figures.[38] We will return to this image below when we discuss the triangular symbolism of the ox-child.

Once more, she has an emotional reaction to the suffering expression in the boy's face, to his "pent-up tension." But this encounter, too, leaves only a brief impression. The child's identity cannot be perceived. The 'dossier,' the file with the knowledge it contains, is in the hands of the older companion. Apparently, the unconscious itself still wants to protect this new content from the eyes of the world.

Protecting a newly emerging content of the unconscious is a central theme in fairy tales and mythological stories. After their first appearance or their first heroic deed, the heroine or hero must normally retreat three times before the wedding or final resolution of the story takes place. Cinderella disappears three times from the court before the prince finally finds her again. The hero who, with the help of an animal or magical figure, performs three heroic deeds, disappears immediately afterwards, etc.[39] There are also many tales of dwarves who, unbeknownst to humans,

38 M.-L. von Franz, *The Interpretation of Fairy Tales,* p. 89 f.

39 See R. Abt, *Princess and Magic Horse. Interpretation of three Fairytales.*

do all the work at night. But the moment they realize that they have been observed, they disappear and usually never come back. They represent a playful, creative spirit that can be scared away if it is recognized too eagerly or if one tries to nail it down. The meaning behind this protective retreat is that everything can be lost if the world of reason accesses the inner-psychic processes too early – "the creative play of images" can be dishevelled and destroyed by rational considerations and criticism.[40]

Imagine if one were to encounter an animal-child like this on the street! It would draw a crowd who would immediately study it, size it up, photograph it, film it. In the past, physically handicapped people were exhibited for money.[41] Naturally, this was terrible for those poor souls and most often they died young. The symbolic life, too, can be similarly destroyed by analysing it too early, Marie-Louise von Franz explains.[42] As the goal, according to the dream, is to somehow unite the seemingly utterly irreconcilable opposites of unconscious, creative energy with consciousness, a different approach is called for here. The dream, then, is dealing with a general and profound psychological problem that has yet to be intellectually grasped. Sometimes one must passively observe over a period of time what the unconscious processes bring up, without immediately wanting to know what it means. Then follows the third scene in the park.

A brief coming together of the opposites of the upper and lower world is then described. The boy is now a small child who the dreamer holds in her arms and studies up close. When her emotional reaction to such a strange, unconscious dream image is honest, neither devaluing it or quickly forgetting it, then it can suddenly reveal itself from close up, and both parties grow calm. We know this feeling: after a successful dream interpretation, we suddenly feel a kind of inner peace and security, even if our problem has not yet been solved. The opposites of one's conscious effort and one's unconscious life have momentarily come closer together. Something of this mysterious, unconscious world becomes briefly palpable.

40 C. G. Jung, *Symbols of Transformation,* [CW 5], § 186.

41 E. Hasler, *Der Riese im Baum.*

42 M.-L. von Franz, *The Interpretation of Fairy Tales,* p. 89.

The dreamer now notices the child's curly hair, and an inverted triangle of hair at the base of his head that resembles pubic hair. From it rises a strange but not unpleasant odour, like ozone and sulphur, the dream says. The child is soothed in her arms. It even falls briefly asleep.

Next to her on the bench sits a woman who thinks that this triangle on the child's head is unpleasant and creepy. The dreamer puts her in her place by looking her straight in the eye. This woman is an aspect of the dreamer's own shadow. She represents her own conventional doubts and disconcertment at this strange apparition from the unconscious. The dreamer must put her in her place by giving her an intense look – by looking at what she sees. The dream is indicating that she must look her own shadow in the eye; she must fasten her eyes upon it, meaning, she must realize it consciously, for it could disturb her relationship with her unconscious. She must pay close attention to it! Even if, initially, it is completely beyond her understanding, this strange, incomprehensible dream image must be accepted without any ifs or buts as something that has chosen to reveal itself from the depths of the collective unconscious.

Let's take a step back. As we saw earlier, the ox face indicates that the boy originates from the instinctive level of the maternal cow. It is a child of the cow! The latter, as we now know, symbolically embodies the archetype of the Great Nature Mother. Within the psyche, this archetype represents the unconscious maternal foundation of all the driving forces of an animal nature. This is why all the mythological Great Nature Mothers are also mistresses of the animals, or they have an animal companion. Animals symbolize the driving force that, in humans, is expressed in impulses, affects, and emotions that have a high energetic potential. Just as we little humans have nothing that we might use to fight off a tiger, with its teeth and claws, in the wild, we also have nothing to oppose these driving forces within, which can overwhelm and override our conscious defenses at any time.

In the dreams we discussed earlier, we saw that instinctual nature also has a kind of purposefulness. Unconscious complexes, which in dreams may take the form of animals, seem to want to develop toward consciousness, for they push themselves, somewhat unpleasantly, into consciousness. When someone upsets us by reacting in a complex and irrational way, or when we ourselves are seized by unreasonable emotions, we prefer not to admit that there could be a purpose behind it on the part of the unconscious.

To what do we accord a kind of intentional purposefulness in the psyche? We have already dealt with this question in the dream of the cow birth. There we talked of a spirit of nature existing in the realm of the unconscious. But what about the spirit which finds expression in learned, intellectual treatises and books? Marie-Louise von Franz explains that we cannot describe spirit in and of itself. «We can observe in the psyche an activity which creates order and therefore assume that something is the source of this activity; that something is what we call spirit.» She describes spirit as «that element which appears in the psyche as a manifestation of order, and which might also appear in matter in the same way.»[43] This meaningful order in both inner and outer nature has always been perceived as something miraculous, something that exceeds our understanding, even today. The contemplative illuminations and visions of the saints were also thought to be the work of a divine spirit. Authentic religious feeling and spirit went hand in hand.

Today, in the Christian realm, spirit has become an imagined male God who resides in heavenly, spiritual spheres. Because of the loss of a religious view of the world in our time, spirit is now predominantly seen as mind and intellect. Having lost any sense of all human spirit originating within unconscious nature, we now overestimate consciousness. This intellectual, modern spirit has nothing to do with feelings or sacred reverence toward the invisible! Rather it feels empowered to every kind of outrage in an infinite number of ideological disguises. Religious feeling can be recognized in some perverted kind of spiritual obsession which echoes the religious zealots of past centuries. Today, we recognize these tendencies in the intolerant, world-improving ideas which are proclaimed with religious fervour by those who believe themselves to be the sole bearers of the truth. In this guise, our inner spirit has become a treacherous seducer.

The spiritual aspect of instinctual nature has largely disappeared. The rapidly increasing mechanization and digitalization of our environment, the media's constant bombardment with news from all over the

43 M.-L. von Franz, *The Psychological Meaning of Redemption Motifs in Fairytales*, p. 49.

world, and our ubiquitous materialism make any mention of there being an unconscious highly dubious. We need to realize that this unconscious has been suppressed, but not put out of action. How this plays out, and how we deal with the consequences of this unhealthy, one-sided extraversion, is the subject of modern depth psychology today. All of C. G. Jung's work is about shedding light on the importance of psychic facts because the loss or suppression and disregard of the natural realm of the spirit greatly influences our whole world view, and how we behave in our culture and society. This collective problem gives rise to archetypal, compensatory dreams like that of the ox-child.

It was C. G. Jung who showed that over the centuries, in compensation to the official, ecclesiastical Christian dogma, philosophers and introverted thinkers went to great lengths to find this natural, spiritual dimension. As mentioned earlier, the experiments of ancient alchemists were an attempt on their part to find the spirit of nature in substances and matter. They described their findings with a great number of names and images. Their fantasies, visions, and hypothetical models of thought, with which they tried to approach the secret contained within matter, were later found to be either lacking or erroneous and they were accordingly rejected or demonized by natural scientists.[44]

But Jung realized that in the works of the great alchemists, in their strange and incomprehensible language and curious imagery, the entire undervalued realm of psychic nature is to be found, the same realm we encounter in our dreams, fantasies and visions, most often in a very peculiar way. In his work with people and through his observation of contemporary events, Jung felt the urgent need to reach some better understanding of the soul's language, which is a symbolic one. We can decipher it to some extent only if we can unlock the symbols and translate them into contemporary psychological terms and descriptions of what is unfolding within the soul. Today, alchemical images and ideas form a bridge for us to understand dream symbols.

Let us now try to understand the image of the mysterious ox-child against the background of alchemy. The dream itself provides us with the

44 M.-L. von Franz, *C. G. Jung. His Myth in Our Time*, p.106 ff.

first clue that can lead us further. It is the triangle of hair, reminiscent of pubic hair, which emits a strange odour of ozone and sulphur. This 'chemical' image already seems to point toward alchemy!

We know now that ozone is a molecule made up of oxygen atoms; it is a colourless, slightly bluish gas with a characteristic odour. In the ozone layer of the stratosphere, oxygen (O_2) is converted into ozone (O_3) by the ultraviolet radiation of the sun. The ozone layer above our earth protects nature and humans from the harmful (UV-C) radiation of the sun. Sulphur, on the other hand, reaches the earth's surface from volcanic eruptions at great depths. Sulphur compounds are found in numerous minerals, but also in plants, animals, and humans.

To illuminate the dream content, we need to understand the symbolic meaning of sulphur and ozone. Sulphur and ozone correspond to the *sulphur* and *aer* (air, wind, pneuma) in the symbolic, 'chemical' language of alchemy. Many of the substances that were used by the alchemists in their experiments which they thought of as being 'chemical' by nature, we no longer think of as chemical today. They were often a part of a projection of pairs of opposites, for example of light/heavy, invisible/visible, etc.[45] In alchemical terms, air and sulphur were opposites, like heaven and hell. *Air* is the upper, spiritual, invisible component that stands in contrast to the yellow sulphur of the earthy, dark, instinctual world. Sulphur has so many meanings in both chemistry and alchemy that we can only hint at what it might mean in connection with our dream. It was one of the most popular substances used by the alchemists.[46] They thought of it as the sulphurous fires of hell, and as a potent, masculine substance.[47]

The dream specifically refers to the strange smell of the two substances. Air is odourless. The ozone of the dream, on the other hand, has a specific odour. It is therefore an appropriate symbol for a spiritual substance that stands in contrast to earthy and compact sulphur. As a gas, (SH_2), sulphur emits a nauseating smell of rotten eggs, which, in the past, was generally held to be the smell of the devil. However, when the two substances combine in the dream, their smell is not offensive. A certain

45 C. G. Jung, *Psychology and Alchemy,* [CW 12], § 398.

46 Ibid., § 401.

47 Ibid., § 470.

odour or scent often accompanies the appearance of an otherworldly power – a god or goddess. The dream is again indicating the special, numinous nature of this child.

On his head, united in a triangle, are the alchemical opposites of aer and sulphur. It is a triangle of curled hair, reminiscent of pubic hair. This might indicate its lower, libidinal nature that has its origins in a layer of the psyche from which our involuntary, instinctual behaviour, including sexuality, comes. It is out of this realm that this strange odour of the two opposing agents emanates. If the dream chooses such an image, we must assume it has a special significance and ask ourselves what this could be saying about the ox-faced child? Alchemy gives us a clue. In alchemical images, sulphur is represented, for instance, as a triangle or as a triangle on a cross.[48]

The trinity points to underworldly deities, for example, the three Norse goddesses of fate, the Norns, the triple underworld goddess Hecate of Greek philosophy, or the Celtic matres or matronae, etc. There are innumerable examples. We find the number three particularly in the "spirit of the substance" that the alchemists were seeking, for example, in the god Mercurius, who was called and depicted as *tricephalous*. In the illustration above[49], he is depicted as a king with three faces and as a triangle between the sun and the moon. Mercurius is also about a «tricephalous (threefold) serpent, or a triunity (a three-unity) par excellence,» as Jung points out.[50]

The smell of *sulphur* and *aer*, in which these opposing substances are united, also points to Mercurius, for, in alchemy, Mercurius is the unifier, the one who can bring together the opposites in nature. He is always described as a paradox containing the most irreconcilable opposites, for example as a "stone carried by the wind," or as the "physically made spirit of the world." It is also said of him that he is «shining bright and burning hot, heavier than metal and lighter than air.»[51] He is simultaneously fire and water, too. Thus, he encompasses all possible opposites. Mercurius is

48 C. G. Jung, *Psychology and Alchemy*, [CW 12], § 70: Fig. 16, and § 456: Fig. 194.

49 Ibid., §70, 16.

50 Ibid., § 31. See also C. G. Jung, *Alchemical Studies,* [CW 13], § 270. (Mercurius as a one-unity and three-unity.)

51 See C. G. Jung, "Flying Saucers: A Modern Myth of Things Seen in the Skies," in: *Civilization in Transition,* [CW 10], § 727.

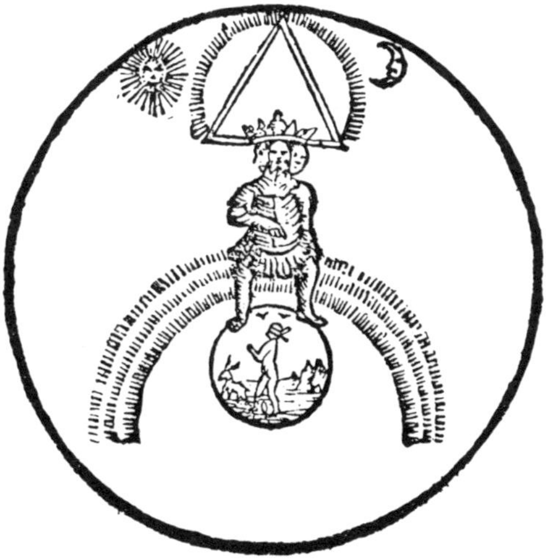

Fig. 9: *Mercurius tricephalus* as anthropos. Beneath his feet, a blindfolded man led by an animal. From: Kelley, *Tractatus de Lapide philosophorum* (1676). In: C. G. Jung, *Psychology and Alchemy,* [CW 12], § 70.

also a son of Great Mother Nature, and he has a special relationship with both the feminine and the moon. He himself is a male-female being. The greatest opposites of good and evil, which Christianity has exacerbated and torn apart, are contained within him. He is said to be good with the good and evil with the evil. This means that it reflects the attitude with which it is approached. He is a spirit of enlightenment, but he is also hellfire and devilish. He is simultaneously both *senex* (the old man) and *puer* (the boy), yet a further pair of opposites.[52]

As Marie-Louise von Franz explains, Mercurius was also referred to in alchemy as a kind of dark god who had become earthly; he had sunk into the depths of the earth and had to be found there again. This

52 C. G. Jung, *Alchemical Studies,* [CW 13], § 276. As *senex*, he approaches Saturn through his kinship with the aged Greek god Hermes. Saturn is «not only a *maleficus* (evildoer), but actually the dwelling-place of the devil himself.» Incidentally, he is also called 'the head' or 'the round.' This resonates with the dream's emphasis on the child's head.

problem has been at the centre of the alchemists' efforts throughout the centuries of alchemical work. Today, in depth psychology, we understand the spirit of Mercurius to be something that lives within each of us. «It is the *numinosum* which, for modern man, appears to have moved into the depths of the earth but in actuality lives in the depths of his own psyche; this is true not only for certain individuals but for very many people.»[53]

But how are we to search for what the god Mercurius meant to the alchemists, for this 'inner god,' today? Mercurius unites all opposites within himself; he has a thousand different names; he is as fleeting and as ambiguous as the symbols of the unconscious themselves. All the allusions, obscurities, and symbolic descriptions relating to him are confusing. In our effort to understand archetypal dream symbols, we often rush hopefully toward any symbol that permits an unambiguous statement, only to realize that its very opposite may be equally true. That is why dream interpretation is never definitive. It leads us into completely unknown realms, where anything can be anything. In the unconscious, all archetypes contaminate each other. Why, then, do we even try to interpret dreams at all?

It is only possible to filter a satisfactory meaning out of this entire *massa confusa* if we engage our evaluative feeling function. Without this conscious effort on our part, dreams remain dreams. The appearance of the afflicted child in our world would be in vain; the compensatory healing impulses from a deeper layer of the soul would sink back into oblivion without leaving a trace.

The suffering of the child in the dream indicates that the unconscious wants to manifest itself, and that there are things in our unknown, spiritual background that we could and should know. The threshold between consciousness and unconsciousness is so strong, however, that it cannot be crossed without danger. Countless myths tell of what happens when the boundary between the human world and the world of the gods is crossed carelessly. Disorientation and confusion follow; there can be a dangerous dissolution of consciousness, even mental illness. We experience our own excessive unconsciousness every time we freak out about something, a

53 M.-L. von Franz, *C.G. Jung: His Myth in Our Time,* p.205. See also p.217: With Mercurius the alchemists produced «not the antitheses of Christ but rather his chthonic counterpart, not a divine man but a fabulous being conforming to the nature of the primordial mother.»

sure sign that we are out of ourselves. Or we can recognize it in every street fight of crowds who are 'aggressively enthusiastic.' This is the devilish, sulphuric aspect of Mercury in action.

Our ox-child, then, clearly shows the mercurial features of an underworldly nature spirit. But he is also born from the cow goddess and still bears her features. Let us recall the double aspect of both nature and spirit in the cow goddess Hathor with her sun disk. We can say that a masculine spirit emerges from the deepest layer of the psyche which can be briefly perceived consciously. In other words, a new spiritual dimension of the female personality is becoming visible. The boy's animal face reveals that this spirit still bears its instinctive form of animal impulses and emotions: it cannot yet find a place in conscious life. This nature spirit in a woman is of a different quality to the rigorous consciousness of men. Perhaps the knowledge that this boy embodies is of a more intuitive nature; perhaps he has the innate instinctive sense that an animal has.[54] He is, therefore, particularly elusive.

In many fairy tales, a future prince or princess, or some other kind of otherworldly being, must be redeemed from its animal form. Psychologically, the point of all these fairy tales is that an enchanted content – one that has fallen into the unconscious – must be brought back into consciousness.[55] Only in human, i.e., conscious, form can it perform its function within the whole of human society or one's personality. The fairy tale is, then, always about a renewal, for example, of a kingdom. It is through the love of a fairy tale hero or heroine which often involves a painstakingly long search that redemption is finally made possible. This dream of the ox-child seems to suggest that the redemption of some aspect of the dreamer's soul is indeed possible. At the end, the dreamer finally does the right thing by lovingly turning toward the child.

On the personal level, this means that as a woman, she takes care of her unconscious masculine intellectual/spiritual side. Today, we call this the animus, which we spoke of earlier. The animus can have all the traits of Mercury, which have been described by the alchemists in so many and

54 M.-L. von Franz, *Archetypal Symbols in Fairytales. The Maiden's Quest* (Vol. 3 of the Collected Works of M.-L. von Franz), p. 2, 4 (§ 2 and § 11).

55 See M.-L. von Franz, *The Psychological Meaning of Redemption Motifs in Fairytales.*

various ways. Like Mercurius himself, the animus is an unknown, fleeting, and utterly unpredictable entity. Like a god, he can be overpowering and creative and full of cold-blooded malice. "To be good with the good and evil with the evil" seems to indicate that it is in the eyes of the Mercurius animus whether one belongs to those who are good or to those who are evil. Of course, this is not to be understood within the context of the Christian moral code of good and evil, which belies an attitude that can readily seduce one into arrogantly believing one is one of the so-called 'good guys,' while all others are not. Two thousand years of Christianity and Church history have provided us with sufficient unpleasant examples of this. No, good and evil in this alchemical dictum depends on whether one turns to the spirit of the unconscious, ponders upon it, and tries to understand it, or whether one chooses to neglect or suppress it. The choice we make can lead either to a creative renewal of life and one's attitude toward it, to spiritual enrichment and the broadening of one's horizons, or it can lead to being opinionated and to narrow-minded obtuseness.[56]

The dark spirit of Mercury cuts a woman off from her femininity and often from her joy of life, leaving her to wander in the backwoods of her own opinions. The modern tendency to make men and women equal on all political and social levels, or even the blurring of the male-female biological and mental differences to promote gender fairness, can be dangerous for the feminine, for it gives the negative animus a wide field to operate in. Instead of being the impetus for an "introverted, spiritual life," and of being «the mediator of creative and religious experience through which life receives its meaning,»[57] the negative animus then goes on the rampage as an opinionated devil in all kinds of destructive, relationship-killing, and instinct-damaging ways in the outer world.

The best thing we women can probably do is to be as aware as we can of all that the animus says without actively opposing his opinions, and then to let him go on his way again, like the ox-child. If we get lost in reproaching ourselves for once again being caught by the negative aspect of the animus, we simply make ourselves and our environment crazy, to

56 See M.-L. von Franz, *The Feminine in Fairy Tales*.

57 See M.-L. von Franz, in: C. G. Jung, *Man and His Symbols.* Chapter: "The Process of Individuation." p. 189–195. And: E. Jung, *Animus and Anima.*

the absolute delight of Mercurius! If, on the other hand, the animus allows us to glimpse the unknown dimensions of the spiritual realm within, we must also accept that this moment is most often brief, and that it will again require a long and devoted effort on our part before he will once more reveal himself in his vivifying form. This is the essence of the redemptive task of the feminine, which we are told in innumerable ways all over the world.

By taking the ox-child in her arms and looking at it lovingly, the dreamer is trying to relate with her feelings to her own creative, imaginative side. This is what we can do when dreams, impulses, fantasies, emotions, and unfamiliar feelings that appear to be asking for integration into our conscious life emerge from within. We simply hold them and take them in, even if, at best, they initially give us only an inkling of what wants to become realized in our attitude towards life, in our relationships, in our plans, and in how we see ourselves.

Since the animus as a creative principle is often secretly connected to the Great Mother – in this instance, the cow goddess –, we are, when dealing with the animus, also dealing with the whole unconscious. This reciprocal relationship between the animus and the maternal, instinctual, archetypal level of the unconscious makes the task of approaching the animus and becoming aware of it so very difficult. He always has one leg, as it were, sunk into the deepest depths of the earth or at the bottom of the sea, where we can never follow.

The visible tension within the ox-child, the new content, shows that this difficulty is mutual, i.e., it also exists for the unconscious. As Jung has mentioned many times, nature, too, suffers in its effort to become conscious. It is, apparently, a painful process for the unconscious, just as it is painful for the ego to be so deeply in the dark. As a rule, no one else can understand our suffering in this regard. Jung explains, «The experience of the unconscious is a personal secret communicable only to very few, and that with difficulty; hence the isolating effect.»[58] On the other hand, it seems that most people can only really be open to the unconscious when they are in a bad way, when they are thrown back on themselves through

58 C. G. Jung, *Psychology and Alchemy,* [CW 12], § 61.

suffering and despair, and conventional solutions no longer promise success. Loneliness is often the precondition for accessing the helpful impulses of the unconscious.

By using the archetypal symbol of the ox-child, the dream takes us beyond the personal into a collective problem of our time. We have already touched upon it with Mercurius, but I would like to deepen our view with the symbol of the divine child, for this is what the dream is about.

As a mythological figure, the archetype of the divine child is so widespread that it would take more than ten volumes to describe it, according to Marie-Louise von Franz. In her view, this archetype comes to the fore when traditional values are being questioned. We have already seen that the divine child is connected to Mercurius, who has been described as both *senex* (the old man) and *puer* (the boy), that is, as a pair of opposites which, in fact, belong together. Marie-Louise von Franz interprets this pair as «the millennia-old wisdom of the unconscious and its eternally youthful power of self-renewal.»[59] We have spoken of this in connection with the cow-birth of the Buddha-child and the statue of the ancient sage. The mercurial symbol of the ox-child encompasses both.

Mythologically speaking, hooded dwarves in fairy tales and legends also belong within the circle of the divine child or the *puer aeternus.*[60] As mentioned earlier, they are mostly helpful, hidden forces of nature. When the figures of the unconscious appear in this form, we are dealing with psychic energy, with spontaneous, new opportunities and a creative reshaping of life.

But some appearances of the divine child are also ominous.[61] Then, perhaps, they take the form ill-tempered or malicious goblins, like the evil dwarf in the fairy tale of Snow White and Rose Red, or Rumpelstiltskin, and many others. Their psychological equivalents are manifold. In many instances, one can recognize the machinations of the negative animus. In a person, the negative aspect of the divine child can also appear, for example, in the form of an infantile shadow, as something childish that

59 M.-L. von Franz, *Puer Aeternus,* p. 35.

60 C. G. Jung, *Symbols of Transformation,* [CW 5], § 184. «The dwarf motif brings us to the figure of the divine boy, the *puer aeternus.*» See also M.-L. von Franz, *Puer Aeternus.*

61 C. G. Jung, *The Archetypes and the Collective Unconscious* [CW 9/1], § 268 f.

makes us sluggish and dependent, as something that blocks creative renewal. In dreams, then, it is important to pay attention to which face the child is showing; it always contains the most diverse possibilities. It is not always clear which possibility should be lived, for even an infantile, childish variant can perhaps set a new development in motion.[62]

The dreamer takes care of the ox-faced boy, i.e., a supra-personal, creative side of the collective unconscious, in a lovingly patient way. By doing so, the dream says, she is able for a moment to relieve some of the tension and suffering in the child's face. As all contents of the unconscious relate to all other contents of the unconscious on an archetypal level, if one content changes, it might bring about change in all other contents. Perhaps, then, we are right to hope that in some infinitesimal way, the effort that one person makes toward a content as significant as the divine animal-child might reduce the tension within the entire collective unconscious.

This type of tension arises wherever important instinctive and emotional life potentialities are locked away in the unconscious, or are 'bewitched' by a one-sided, rational, conscious attitude. This is dangerous because everything that is repressed in the unconscious turns destructive. When important emotional values of a culture are severed and seem to disappear into the unconscious, tension, strife, and war arise on a collective level. Behind this is the deluding, lying, seductive side of Mercurius. He becomes the spirit of lies, as can be increasingly seen not only in politics, but in all areas of life and relationships. From the standpoint of depth psychology, this is precisely the dangerous situation we find ourselves in today.

To summarize, we have tried to illuminate the dream symbol of the ox-child by putting it into a mythological context. We have seen that this child – this archetype of renewal – has manifested as a symbol in the dreamer's unconscious because of the collective spiritual emergency of our time. Such a divine child represents an attempt on the part of the unconscious to bring about a «new creative religious attitude and a renewal of cultural creativity,»[63] a creative renewal at a time of decay in the traditional spirit of our culture, as Marie-Louise von Franz states in her

62 See M.-L. von Franz, *Puer Aeternus*, p. 35.

63 Ibid., p. 35.

seminal book *Puer Aeternus*. Thus, the background to the problem of an entire age can present itself in a single dream!

The encounter with this spirit of nature when it surfaces is a brief but meaningful experience, one that gives the dreamer an inkling of something underworldly which, as the dream itself says, disappears again in an instant. In the final, fourth part of the dream, the ox-child leaves the upper level of the conscious world. As an artist, it will be of crucial importance for the dreamer's mental balance and spiritual development to allow unconscious images to continue to surface, and to give them creative form. To achieve this, she will, as it were, need the patience and loving devotion of a nurturing cow!

Even though it remains an inexhaustible theme I would like to close this chapter on the cow with this big dream of the ox-child. We shall now turn our attention to a completely different animal, one that will require us to take a huge leap into the water: the octopus.

Part II

The Octopus

Fig. 10: Octopus. Photo Getty Images.

How did I get from the cow to the octopus, the eight-armed creature of the sea? Anything is possible in the unconscious, and the symbols it produces in dreams appear in the most seemingly bizarre and absurd contexts. For the unconscious, then, it is not a problem to jump from cow to octopus! Whether a picture, a symbol, or anything else that emerges from this universal layer of the psyche particularly appeals, fascinates, repels, or occupies us is simply a question of one's own personal feeling. And I am quite taken with the octopus!

I have been fascinated by the octopus for a long time. I was struck by various reports from keepers and scientists involved in observing octopuses in captivity. I found the South African documentary film "My Octopus Teacher" ("Mein Lehrer der Krake") by Craig Foster particularly moving.[64] Diving daily over months, Foster was able to establish a relationship to an octopus, which, if our due diligence as scientists did not forbid such a view in the first place, could be seen as involving elements of 'conscious awareness' on the part of the octopus. Not only Foster but innumerable researchers have directed all their efforts to the study of this strange sea creature.[65] Literature on this subject is already vast!

We usually place this inconspicuous animal somewhere between jellyfish, sea cucumbers, and crabs. We may have already encountered it at the fish market or on a plate. But what is the great fascination behind the octopus that motivates so many to go to such great lengths to both observe and document their research? As depth psychologists, when we ask ourselves this question on any subject, we always assume that in such a case something within our psyche is moved, as it were, by some energetic undercurrent, by some factor in the unconscious psyche, which makes its presence felt in symbolic form by 'latching on', if you like, to an external, suitable object. This makes the octopus a symbol of something that is a part of us. When at the end of the film Foster says that we are not only a part of nature, but that we "are nature" – a distinction he feels

64 J. Reed and C. Foster: *My Octopus Teacher.* Directed and written by P. Ehrlich and J. Reed, produced by C. Foster, starring C. Foster and T. Foster, co-produced by Netflix, 2020.

65 One example among many: P. Godfrey-Smith, *Other Minds: The Octopus and the Evolution of Intelligent Life.* I would also like to mention a concisely written paper that references psychology: B. Wagner: *Der Octopus.* Symbolarbeit am C.G. Jung Institut, Küsnacht 2000 (not published).

is of central importance –, he is aptly expressing how we identify some inner image with some outer object, something inner with outer nature. This connection that might be hard to imagine is portrayed in a dream of a 40-year-old woman, and it is with this dream that I would like to open our reflections upon the octopus.

Dream 6: The two octopuses in the sea

I see photos in which I suddenly recognize myself. I am underwater, diving with octopuses. I am sitting on the bottom of the sea with a small, dark red octopus on my lap; a much larger one is sitting next to us. I am playing with one of its arms. I experience the whole thing as if it were a movie. Apparently, I have forgotten this episode, but I am now slowly remembering it. I wonder why I was so brave. Something could have happened: animals are unpredictable, especially those we know so little about. I look very beautiful in the photo, a little like a queen.

To plumb even a little of the depth of this dream, let us first take a closer look at some of the many facets of the octopus as a living creature.

Unlike other cephalopods, such as the ten-armed cuttlefish or squid, many anecdotes and observations about the octopus refer to its intelligence, its inventiveness, and even to its "mischievous and cunning nature."[66] In captivity, octopuses are quite capable of adapting to the situation they find themselves in and of interacting with humans. They recognize people and react accordingly, even spraying unwanted visitors with a jet of water. Laboratory octopuses are extremely inventive when it comes to manipulating their water tank when no one is watching, or opening the lid of a sealed jar from the outside – or even the inside – to get at food. Observations of octopuses in the wild have revealed how they make good use of foreign objects. In 2009, researchers in Indonesia documented octopuses dragging two halves of a coconut shell around with them to use as a portable shelter. With visible effort, the animals tucked the interlocked halves beneath their bodies, and, with stiff arms, they clambered over the sandy seabed until they eventually assembled them

66 P.. Godfrey -Smith, *Other Minds. The Octopus and the Evolution of intelligent Life,* p.42.

into a whole and climb inside.[67] Craig Foster observed how, when it was in danger of being eaten by a shark, an octopus camouflaged itself by placing empty shells all around, making itself almost indistinguishable from the surrounding coral. Another attached itself to the back of the shark that was pursuing it, making it impossible for the shark to eat it. According to Godfrey-Smith, octopuses are smart, for they are curious, adaptable, adventurous, and playful.[68] «Only intelligent animals play, birds like crows and parrots, primates like monkeys and chimps, dogs and humans.»[69] To adapt to its surroundings and any current dangerous situation, the octopus can, within seconds, spontaneously change into any conceivable shape in a dazzling array of colours. It can also confuse its enemies by adopting the form, colour, and pattern of other marine animals. An octopus's mood can be readily recognized by its colour: when at rest, it is pale, for example, but when angry or excited, it can become red.[70]

Octopuses have a further astonishing characteristic that is otherwise attributed to more highly developed animals, such as dogs, namely the ability to establish a relationship with a person that goes beyond simply reacting, and the performance of tricks. This has been witnessed, for example, by patient animal keepers and regular visitors to zoos and laboratories.[71] What Craig Foster achieved, for example, I found most remarkable: after spending a long time getting to know an octopus living in the wild in the sea, he was able to elicit a reaction from the animal which could only be interpreted as sympathy or trust.[72]

We need to bear in mind that octopuses, or cephalopods, which are said to be as docile as dogs, go back to primeval times – indeed, to the very origins of life. They are, if you like, living fossils, for cephalopods and other molluscs have been creatures of the sea for about 164 million years;

67 S. Montgomery, *The Soul of an Octopus. An Exploration into the Wonder of Consciousness*, p. 94.

68 P. Godfrey-Smith, *Other Minds,* p.64.

69 S. Montgomery, *The Soul of an Octopus,* op. cit., p. 54.

70 R. Ellis, *Seeungeheuer, Mythen, Fabeln und Fakten,* p. 277.

71 See S. Montgomery, *The Soul of an Octopus.* op. cit.

72 At the end of the film *My Octopus Teacher,* Foster's final encounter with the octopus saw the octopus going into his arms, 'attaching' itself to his chest, and stroking Foster's face with one arm.

Fig. 11: Craig with his Octopus. From the South African documentary "My Octopus Teacher."

fish and other vertebrates arose much later. Perhaps our last common ancestor with the octopus was some kind of millimetre-sized flattened worm living in the ocean about 600 million years ago. The branches of evolution then separated. Like snails and clams, octopuses are a subgroup of molluscs. They, however, evolved an extensive nervous system and the ability to behave in ways that are very different from other invertebrates. The cephalopods are «an independent experiment in the evolution of large brains and complex behaviours. If we can make contact with cephalopods as sentient beings, it is not because of a shared history, not because of kinship, but because evolution built minds twice over. This is probably the closest we will come to meeting an intelligent alien,» says Godfrey Smith. For a competent scientist to compare cephalopods like the octopus to 'an intelligent alien' is quite remarkable![73]

With approximately the same number of neurons as smaller mammals, the nervous system of an octopus resembles, for example,

73 P. Godfrey-Smith, *Other Minds,* p. 9.

that of dogs. But the structural layout of an octopus' nervous system is fundamentally different: it is less centralized and more distributed throughout its entire body than that of vertebrates. There are almost twice as many neurons in an octopus' arms than there are in its brain. Having their own sensors, its arms can not only feel, but also smell or taste.[74] Which is why, according to Godfrey-Smith, the octopus' intelligent and flexible behaviour cannot be explained by the size of its brain and the number of its neurons. From an evolutionary point of view, certain 'intelligent' skills are advantageous. But beyond that, the octopus displays a kind of surprising, inventive, and curious behaviour that poses a great puzzle to researchers. «Apparently, the octopus has some kind of mental surplus.»[75] And if, as it seems, an octopus, who has remained unchanged for over 500 million years, can connect 'emotionally' (if I may use that term anthropomorphically here) to the person or thing it is facing, then the conclusion for depth psychology could be that within this unique experiment on the part of evolution there might exist a kind of natural spirit. And if so, would it be too far-fetched to imagine that there is also something like an eros function inherent in nature?

This speculation, in fact, coincides with the findings of C. G. Jung's observational research on the 'inner nature' of human beings, on the human psyche, which is also millions of years old. From dreams and other manifestations of the unconscious, Jung found that there is, apparently, a naturally occurring spiritual instance within the psyche that relates to the individual in a way that is both helpful and prospective. We spoke of this earlier in relation to the cow. Nature repeatedly surprises us by having what appears to be a kind of eros toward us, a kind of 'emotional' connection, when, for example, dreams or spontaneous ideas bring up unexpected solutions and guiding intuitions that appear to be aimed at furthering our own development. It is as if there were an instance in the psyche that is deeply interested in us. Anyone who has experienced this 'instance' – or whatever you wish to call it – which, through dreams, fantasies, ideas, or some other form of expression on the part of the unconscious, has meaningfully influenced their life, has no doubt about this.

74 Ibid., p. 67.
75 Ibid., p. 73.

Fig.12: Octopus attacks a ship. According to Denys de Montfort.

Until now, we have approached the phenomenon of the cephalopods, particularly the octopus, from the angle of evolution. From observatory evidence, we have noted their amazing appearance and behaviour. But humans have always had a special relationship with this largely unknown, 'alien' creature, a relationship that is revealed in a wealth of fantastic ideas, in stories and in symbolic images. When, as depth psychologists, we seek to illuminate and understand the octopus as a dream image, this wealth of material is as important to us as any description of the real animal. By looking at the ideas humans have formed around this strange creature, around this experiment of nature in emergent consciousness, we might better understand something of what it represents in us, in our psyche, and in our dreams.

With their sucker-lined arms, both eight-armed octopuses and ten-armed squids have always evoked the terrifying image of creatures

Fig. 13: Blue-ringed octopus

that grab and pull their prey down into the depths, or even swallow them whole. But octopuses are, in fact, quite peaceful animals, as are the legendary giant squids which can grow up to 23 metres long, and about which seaman have spun many a fearsome tale.

With a single head in the middle of its body and a further eight heads on long necks, the Hydra of Lerna, that guards the entrance to the realm of the dead and which Heracles had to defeat, resembles an octopus. Like the Hydra, the Scylla is a monster reminiscent of a giant squid. It is an embodiment of very great evil,[76] which has very little to do with squids and a great deal with the unconscious of humankind. Human consciousness is a recent achievement in human history, and it is constantly at risk of being swallowed up again by the threatening dark of the unconscious. The octopus, though a peaceful and mischievous creature, has come to symbolize this danger. There is, in fact, only one truly dangerous species of octopus and that is the relatively small 'blue-ringed octopus' that lives off the coast of Australia, whose venomous bite can, indeed, kill a human.

76 J. Chevalier, A. Gheerbrant, *Dictionnaire des Symboles,* "Pieuvre". And: R. Caillois, *Der Krake,* p. 103.

The octopus and its entwining arms came to be associated with the sensual and the sexual, particularly in the Christian era. Considered destructive and deceptive, it was thought to be lascivious. For the ancient Church Fathers, the octopus symbolized debauchery and diabolical. It was also associated with the traitor Judas, for, like Judas, the octopus would first 'embrace' its victims, only to deviously kill them afterwards. At a time when natural science still largely fed on fantastic tales, octopuses were described as murderous, treacherous creatures that caused violent whirlpools in the sea, thereby sinking both ships and people.[77] By the 19th century, however, the octopus became increasingly seen as a symbolic personification of both the creative and the destructive spirit of humankind. Nevertheless, especially in Romanticism, and in stories, poetry and more recently, in film, there was still this notion of a sea monster or giant squid which carried the projection of evil.[78]

Like any archetypal symbol, however, the octopus also has decidedly positive sides. From the indigenous people of Fiji in the South Pacific, who, from experience, probably feel more benevolently towards the octopus, comes the following story, "The Battle of the Shark and the Octopus." In it, an octopus called Rokobakaniceva fights the great shark god Dakuwaqa who, until then, had never been defeated. But after being defeated by the octopus, the shark god must promise to spare any island people who are shipwrecked from that time on. The shark god then becomes the protector of those who are shipwrecked, and from then on, a bond of friendship exists between the people of the octopus Rokobakaniceva and the land of the great Dakuwaqa. According to the story, an imprint of the octopus can still be seen in a rock.[79]

Octopuses have also been attributed healing powers. When in danger, octopuses, squid, and cuttlefish have an ink sac that they can squirt at their enemies. This ink has been used for healing purposes since ancient times. Cuttlefish ink is used as a remedy in homeopathy today. The octopus's ability to regrow an arm once bitten-off, so splendidly shown in the film by Craig Foster, has undoubtedly impressed a lot of people. Its ability to

77 R. Callois, *Der Krake,* p. 27.

78 See this passage with B. Wagner, *Octopus*, p. 10 ff. And: R. Caillois, p. 100 f.

79 A.W. Reed, *Myths and Legends of Fiji,* p. 45 f.

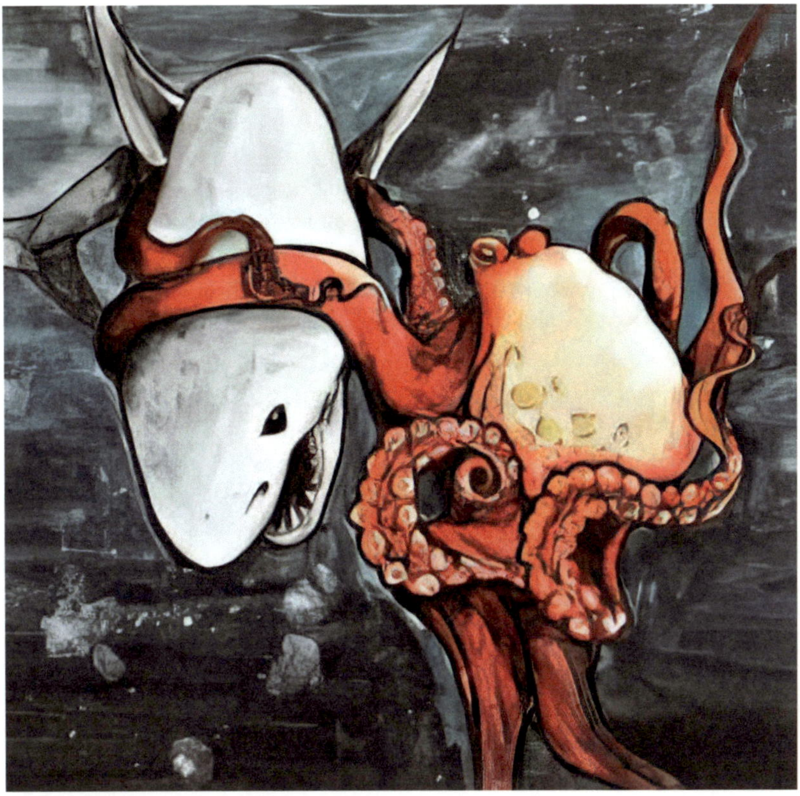

Fig. 14: Dakuwaqwa, the shark god doing battle with the octopus. In: Island Time. *The Octopus – A Fijian Legend.*

renew itself, its adaptability, and its amazing capacity to imaginatively change its colour have contributed to the octopus becoming an image of the alchemical figure of Hermes-Mercurius. As the personification of the trickster spirit of the unconscious, the latter can always unexpectedly and spontaneously upset old habits and entrenched views. The octopus's ability to avoid being caught by playing tricks and deceiving fishermen led Aristotle to describe it as clever. Its ability to change its colour when required led Plutarch, on the other hand, to think of it as cunning.

Naturally a trickster, an octopus in dreams can perform the function of dissolving a hardened consciousness, thereby providing an opening for the inflow of creative content.[80] We can assume that the creative aspect of the octopus will play a central role in the dreams that follow. But more about that later.

For the alchemical philosophers, the octopus was a fitting image to describe certain aspects of the philosopher's stone, the goal of the alchemical opus.[81] To their mind, its eight arms alone – a double four – made it a symbol of divine wholeness. Four is the basis of our orientation in the outer world, for example the four cardinal directions, the four seasons, the four cycles of the moon [full and new moon, waxing and waning moon].[82] Thus, despite its multiformity and its ability to constantly change, the octopus stands not only for an incomprehensible, slippery, suction-cup-wielding chaos, but also for bringing order. It is a creature that can bring many opposing and independent 'moving parts' into a purposeful whole. As we have seen, Jung named this central, ordering instance in the psyche the self – the same instance the ancient philosophers never tired of describing by an infinite number of symbolic images.

From this woefully short and incomplete overview, which by no means does justice to the miraculous being of the octopus, we can nevertheless glean some important points: On the one hand, the octopus has become a projection carrier for all kinds of unconscious, shadow characteristics and drives of both a positive and negative nature, and, on the other hand, it has become a symbol for the centring, ordering, and self-renewing creative power that dwells within the depth of the unconscious – an essential aspect of the self. Now that we know and can learn more about the octopus, we understand that, in the dreams of people today, it embodies a very deep, archetypal layer of the psyche, which, on its own initiative, is able to establish contact with consciousness. Like the octopus itself, the impulses that emerge from this layer appear strange, unexpected, colourful, playful, intelligent, and, in some circumstances, threatening to

80 See M.-L. von Franz, *Creation Myths,* p. 82.

81 M.-L. von Franz's commentary on Ibn Umail, *Kitāb Ḥall ar-Rumūz, Book of the Explanation of the Symbols.* p. 163, CALA I A., ed. by Theodor Abt.

82 See Th. Abt, *Introduction to Picture Interpretation,* p. 127 ff.

us, but – and this is quite amazing – they relate to us! If we try to engage with them, we may even come to understand their intent. The dream above speaks of this, and I am taking the liberty of repeating it here:

I see photos in which I suddenly recognize myself. I am underwater, diving with octopuses. I am sitting on the bottom of the sea with a small, dark red octopus on my lap; a much larger one is sitting next to us. I am playing with one of its arms. I experience the whole thing as if it were a movie. Apparently, I have forgotten this episode, but I am now slowly remembering it. I wonder why I was so brave. Something could have happened: animals are unpredictable, especially those we know so little about. I look very beautiful in the photo, a little like a queen.

With the help of photos, the dreamer's memory comes to life (like a film). We do not know her life circumstances at that time. But apparently this memory takes her back to a time when she was as if "on the bottom of the sea," that is, far from her ordinary world, in a state of 'immersion' out of which creative ideas arise. There, the dream says, she met the two octopuses. The small, red one indicates an emotional or excited state, because we usually associate red with fire, with hot emotion and heated affect, but also with blood, heart, warmth, and feeling. Presumably, this little red octopus was a creative impulse that approached consciousness, charged with emotionally-laden possibilities which lie ready within the unconscious. The larger octopus next to it, with whose arm she is playing, is presumably a further, larger, creative potential with new contents and possibilities to be embraced. Initially, it is encountered in a playful way, as is often the case with a truly creative activity. The dream is probably describing a quite introverted act of turning toward these rising fantasies, one that took place in the dreamer's past, and can now be reactivated. This is quite intentional on the part of the unconscious. We do not yet know the why of it, for it has not yet been revealed. We can only feel our way forward as far as the dream itself will take us.

At the end, there is the important sentence: "I look very beautiful in the photo, a little like a queen." What does a queen mean to a woman? Fairy tales are full of queens and kings. Even if our Swiss history shows that we have always steered clear of royalty, nevertheless, even in our country, every girl loves princesses who will one day become the queen.

Though seldom seen, the passing-by of royal carriages and state-coaches still draws crowds to the roadsides. As Jung points out in his discussion of *rex* and *regina* in alchemy, this fascination has to do with the fact that the king and queen embody more than the couple who reign, and who behave in a more or less exemplary manner: behind them stands the whole might and impact of an archetypal symbol.[83] As the regency of the king is granted by the grace of God, as it were, the king is traditionally the visible incarnation of the divine principle, a symbol of the ineffable archetype of the self.[84]

Having just spoken of the octopus as a symbol of the self, we are now saying that the king, too, is a symbol of the self. This is confusing. What or who, then, is the self? We only know that this central, organizing, ineffable but powerful factor in the unconscious psyche has been experienced and described in thousands of ways throughout the ages. The king or queen embody a different aspect of the self from that of the octopus, as we have described it. The king, who by virtue of his 'divine' destiny exercises supreme power in the land, is, in a society or culture, a symbolic representation of the dominant collective attitude or worldview, which emanates from the self. He is the ruling principle of consciousness. The queen, on the other hand, is the «accompanying feminine element – the emotions, feelings, irrational impulses attached to this dominant content.» In our Christian culture, for example, Mary, the "Queen of Heaven" embodies this feminine element.[85] In symbolical terms, if a country is ruled over by both a king and a queen, then the political and intellectual culture is therein upheld by a consensus, by a shared sense of identity. Although Switzerland has neither king nor queen, it may nevertheless serve as a special example of how a small state that encompasses all manner of opposites has never definitively fallen apart throughout its entire 700-year history, because of just such a sense of shared identity among its inhabitants. Through all their crises, there must have been something like an inner, superordinate feeling value in Switzerland which was again and

83 C.G. Jung, *Mysterium coniunctionis I*, [CW 14], chapter 4: "Rex and Regina".

84 M.-L. von Franz, *Interpretation of Fairy Tales,* p. 52.

85 See Ibid., p. 54.

again able to unite the quarrelsome Swiss. This superordinate, feeling value is an embodiment of the collective, feminine aspect of the self.

What, then, do the king and queen represent in the dreams of everyday people? In men, the queen, the feminine principle, has to do with their anima, their spiritual/emotional state. In women, on the other hand, the queen represents a woman's supreme feminine value, an embodiment of her feminine self, which underlies the growth of her inner personality. Feeling almost like a queen, therefore, points to having an inkling about becoming oneself as a woman.

The entire dream portrays a state of creative immersion. The dreamer experiences what can take place within the depths of the unconscious, namely an experience of the self. This is not different to what we know from experiences of the divine told by mystics and saints in many legends and myths, but also in poetry, painting, music, and, indeed, everything that comes from this deep layer of the unconscious. This is what the encounter with the two octopuses on the ocean floor represents. The dreamer is reminded that she must have been 'there' once before. The two octopuses indicate the independent, mischievous, colourful, and always completely unexpected way that the self may choose to manifest from the unconscious.

In the dream, the dreamer feels "a little like a queen." We can understand the queen here as her inner destiny. At the time of the dream, it must have been important for the dreamer to realize this.

Perhaps at that time she was, as it were, sitting "high and dry," a state that happens to us again and again when, in dealing with our everyday lives, we lose touch with the flow of life, with our energy and creative imagination. Dreams often compensate the conscious situation of a dreamer. This dream literally puts the dreamer back into the waters of the unconscious, where unexpected creative impulses are to be found.

A few theoretical considerations seem appropriate here. It would be reasonable to expect the dream to gives us more precise details, more concrete guidelines about the dreamer's life. Since we do not know her personal situation in detail, we can only assume from the archetypal symbolism that the dream has to do with a creative problem. This intentional reticence on the part of the author applies by and large to all the dreams in this book. As Marie-Louise von Franz explains, a dream interpretation «is never absolutely 'right,' but will have, to a greater or lesser degree, a 'clarifying' or 'illuminating' and enlivening effect. Indeed, the interpretation has no goal beyond that of reconnecting consciousness with the source of energy, which is the archetype.»[86] In the case of archetypal dreams, which are particularly emotional or repetitive, there is the great temptation to resolutely reduce the dream to the personal level, thereby missing out on any reconnection to this source of power.

But don't we need to understand the relationship of the archetypal to the personal in order to grasp the meaning of these dreams? Jung's response is that an archetype is never «[…] a mere name, word, or concept […] an exchangeable coin in intellectual commerce. […] It is a piece of life, an image connected with the living individual by the bridge of emotion.»[87] In personal analysis, where we can consider the feelings and reactions of the analysand, we try to get a sense of this delicate relationship between the archetypal and personal realm. We do this because, as von Franz tells us, «A merely intellectual interpretation is never satisfactory, because the feeling-value of the archetypal content is just as important as its understanding.»[88] «[Archetypes] gain life and meaning only when you try to learn about their numinosity, their relationship to the living individual.»[89] For this reason, our attempt at interpreting archetypal dreams of animals can be no more than of limited assistance to understanding individual dreams.

Assumptions about the initial situation are possible (for example the dreamer's listlessness, her desperate feelings of meaninglessness and her search for meaning – asking herself where she should look for meaning, or having no idea where she might begin with some form of creative work, all the while feeling worthless – a sense of "I can't do that!" or something similar), but the dreamer needs to be able to confirm or reject these assumptions in a personal conversation. In the colourful language of this dream, we recognize that above all it could ultimately be about the

86 M.-L. von Franz, *C. G. Jung. His Myth in Our Time,* p. 131.

87 C.G. Jung, "Symbols and the Interpretation of Dreams," in: *The Symbolic Life,* [CW 18], § 589.

88 M.-L. von Franz, *C. G. Jung. His Myth in Our Time,* p. 131.

89 C.G. Jung, "Symbols and the Interpretation of Dreams," in: *The Symbolic Life,* [CW 18], § 590, see there also chapter "The Archetype in Dream Symbolism," § 521–559.

realization of her queen-self, and that there is a "creative octopus" instance in the unconscious that seems to play an essential role in this process. The whole dream also conveys a particularly impressive emotional tone, which we must respect beyond any interpretation.

Sometimes, when we are unable to identify what has brought about an impressive dream, or when the meaning of a dream remains hidden in the dark, we must rein in our impatience. In those moments, it is simply a matter of waiting for the meaning of the dream to reveal itself, or for an external event to unfold that explains the dream, for example, an event still hidden in the future that the unconscious is already preoccupied with.[90] As a rule, it is best, then, if we begin our interpretation with a modest "It seems as if …!"

When pondering the meaning of dreams, much of what the dream may still contain must be put aside. Every dream has many levels, as it were! Just how many levels it might have can be seen in Jung's *Dream Seminars* where his work on a single dream, or dream series, runs to hundreds of pages![91]

The above dream was not the last dream our dreamer was to have of an octopus. About a year later, it made a further appearance.

Dream 7: The Octopus / Crab in Prison

I am in a prison, being led by the guards along a corridor (that is deep within the building) to a cell. They open the door. Inside, it is pitch black. Once my eyes have adjusted somewhat to the darkness, I see an animal on the floor. It is a cross between an octopus and a crab, about half a metre long. It moves unpredictably, at once swiftly, and then it pauses; it seems to be sizing me up. As it moves toward the door, I think to myself that under no circumstances may I let it escape. I suddenly recall stories from the octopus book in which the author relates how animals managed to break out of their prisons, only to then die miserably, drying up because they need water, or in some other way. I certainly don't want that to happen to this animal. I am also aware of how clever this creature is. Once it is

90 Ibid., § 543.

91 See for example C. G. Jung, *Dream Analysis Seminar.*

outside, we will have little chance of recapturing it. I also realize that I don't want to jam it by closing the door too quickly, especially in the moment it tries to escape. I start to close the door slowly, hoping that I will succeed and that nothing will happen to the animal. While doing this, I am also thinking that I would like to take it and save it. Just how I could do that is not clear to me, because it has crab claws and could hurt me. After all, it doesn't know that I am well disposed towards it.

The dreamer's associations revealed that at the time she did, indeed, feel somewhat locked in; it was a dark time for her. In the dream, she is being led into the cell by guards. Male figures who hinder or imprison the feminine in dreams usually have to do with thoughts and judgments that constrict, unsettle, and keep a woman from being in life. But often it is precisely when we feel locked up, unhappy, and see no future perspective that we are offered the chance of getting a peek at what is going on in the unconscious. Is this, then, a *felix culpa* on the part of the animus?

It is again about the octopus, the creative potential of the dreamer that can take on many forms. But now it is locked up and has become more aggressive. The crab claws of the dream are more dangerous than the beak of an octopus. (Octopuses have a hard beak, like a parrot, which can easily crack hard shells.) This is in line with the psychological experience that a person's unused or forgotten creative potential is dangerous and can cause great psychic damage. Some people are called upon to be creative. It is, so to speak, their vocation. But if one has such a talent and for some reason cannot or will not deal with it, or if one's personality is simply too weak to do so, then, as Marie-Louise von Franz explains, that person is in danger of suffering some form of mental illness or even death. If, on the other hand, a person is healthy and strong, he or she can live on both levels, as it were – they can conform and function in the world while remaining in touch with their inner, 'eternal' personality.[92]

On crabs with hard shells, the dreamer associates being armoured, being defensive, withdrawal, introversion, and being connected to her own inner images. She now finds herself in a real conflict. Should she let the octopus/crab out of prison, thereby risking that it might die? Or should

92 M.-L. von Franz, *Archetypal Patterns in Fairy Tales,* p. 150.

she keep it in by carefully closing the door? Every creative person has this conflict. If you let your intuitions and ideas out too soon, you easily lose contact with the flow of energy from the unconscious, out of which they arose. If, on the other hand, you forget or repress them, if you do not pay attention to them, or feel incapable of dealing with them, you may become distraught and depressed, a state in which nothing works at all. Sometimes, we have a creative impulse, an idea, an inspiration, but it slips away all too easily, before we can fully grasp it. To stay with the dream image: If it has already forced its way out of the open prison door, it is difficult to get it back inside without harming it. If our door of introversion is too open, for example, if we talk to someone about a project, an idea, a fantasy, about inner images too soon, they can easily be harmed. Before we know it, an unformed content is outside, where, even though we are still involved with it, it may nevertheless then be criticized and talked about by others. Instead of being able to grow and develop without disturbance, it then becomes hemmed in and 'jammed', as it were. Even well-meaning criticism can bring one's entire creative flow to a standstill.

Sometimes, it seems as if the unconscious deliberately puts us in prison, into the misery of being locked up, into a state of introversion which our friends fail to understand, and in which we suffer, for we have no clue about what good may come of it all. Every creative human being also has the urge and the need to go out, to interact and achieve things, to bring something new to life and to receive recognition for it. Drive and motivation are not negative, providing we do not "open the door too wide" and lose ourselves in extraversion, in overestimating ourselves, in feelings of inferiority, in being too dependent on the judgment of others, in ambition and superficiality etc. All the above put us in danger of harming the vulnerable and still quite incomprehensible octopus/crab impulses from the unconscious, and thus, the whole creative process. This is always a serious problem whenever something new approaches consciousness from a deeper level of the unconscious psyche.

Most often there is what the alchemists described as the phase of *nigredo*, an initial period of darkness and disorientation in which one cannot yet see how things will develop. In this phase, one may have to carefully restrain, protect, and nurture unruly, impatient, creative octopus/crab energy that is pushing outward. This octopus/crab creature needs water: one needs to surround these emerging contents again and again with playful imagination, to feed them, as it were, with other unconscious material, so that they can live and grow, thereby reducing their dangerous influence. This requires patience, and then still more patience, sometimes years even, until something seems to change, and the first, thin ray of light penetrates the prison. If we can refrain from wanting to know what will come of it all, the unconscious is suddenly supportive: the prison comes to life. Suddenly, we can put an insight down on paper, or realize an idea; we can paint a picture or set something in motion in some way.

It is up to us to recognize the right moment to open the door, to bring what wants to be created into the light of day and out into life. The right moment for any creative process cannot easily be predicted, and it is often difficult to become creative at the push of a button, to deliver, for example, what is expected of us on time, or to curb our own impatience. How we long to see some kind of result! And finally, we must accept that for all these reasons, there are times when we do not quite fit in to our social environment.

Perhaps it is the octopus, an incomparably colourful, flexible, friendly being from another world and time, which has brought us these problems! An octopus's knowledge is different to our type of conscious knowledge. We can only connect with it if we go down into the water, down to its level. We would need to sink into a kind of dreamy, patient inactivity, as divers do when they sink down and search for an octopus. In order not to drown, however, we need a snorkel or an oxygen bottle, or we must return to the surface from time to time to catch our breath. In this context, our oxygen would be our conscious awareness which, as Jung always underscored, plays a very important role in any encounter with the unconscious. It also plays a vital role if we want to approach the creative potential of the octopus. The real miracle is, however, that it is possible for us to enter into a relationship with the octopus – with the self – at all!

Dreams in which an octopus is the embodiment of evil, where it is threatening, dangerous, devouring, frightening, and unsettling to the dreamer, seem to be common. When we are at war with an animal in dreams, we may assume that we are too unconscious of our own behaviour, of a concept, or of an attitude that is upsetting to this animal within us. As an archetype, it is rare to see the octopus in its positive, creative aspect so clearly represented as it is in the dreams above.

After finishing this chapter, I was ready for this book to be finished. I had no intention of getting involved with a further animal, let alone one as frightening as the snake, which I sensed was lurking somewhere in my psyche. But, as the saying goes, “We suggest, but God directs.” Consequently, I felt compelled to delve into the vast material on one of the most important archetypal animal symbols, and the chapter that follows was thereby born.

Part III

The Snake

Fig. 15: Zeus Mailichios. Relief, marble, circa 400–375 BC.

One day I was hiking with our young children across a steep mountain meadow when one of them gleefully went to pick up a nice, thick stick lying in the grass. It was not a stick, but a snake: an adder. Long before considering whether the snake was poisonous or not, I reacted "from my gut" and pulled my child back. I was reacting out of an irrational, primitive fear that I had no control over. Snakes frighten most people. I suppose few people would not react instinctively with fear to a sudden encounter with a snake. My reaction to the stick – to the snake in the grass – was an involuntary, instinctual human reaction coming from a deep psychic level where mostly only physical reactions are possible – a leap to the side, for example. Thinking and reasoning are completely switched off in those moments.

As snakes lie hidden in the grass or foliage, you never know if you might step on one. That's why, as Jung says, a snake in dreams is often like a warning sign on a road: "Attention! Danger ahead!"[93] We never know if it is poisonous or not.

Snakes often appear in dreams, and they always leave a somewhat threatening, or at least impressive, feeling. There is something 'special' about them that we cannot explain. Sometimes we feel only horror and disgust, but at other times, snakes in dreams can be creatures of beauty that fill us with awe and admiration.

It is typical of snakes to have this double, light-dark aspect. They appear not only in dreams, but also in mythology, in legends, in fairy tales, and in the traditions of humankind. And, of course, the snake appears in the Bible where it embodies the devil who tempts Eve to pluck the apple from the tree of knowledge and is therefore behind Adam and Eve's expulsion from the Garden of Eden. A more positive view of the biblical serpent credits it with triggering humankind's knowledge of good and evil thereby making us aware of our own human nature and of the ambiguous nature of God.[94] Although guilty, it is a *felix culpa* on the part of humankind: the Church still glorifies it in the Easter mass when it is said, «O happy fault! O necessary sin of Adam, which gained for us so great a Redeemer!»

93 C. G. Jung, *The Visions Seminars I, Notes to the Seminar given in 1930–34*, p. 268 f.

94 See E. Hornung's excellent essay: "Söhne der Erde. Schlangen im Diesseits und Jenseits der Ägypter" and A. Schweizer: "Schlangenträume." In: E. Hornung; A. Schweizer, *Die Weisheit der Schlange*.

We encounter this double aspect of good and evil in the snake particularly clearly, for example, in the following dream of a child.

Dream 8: The black-and-white snake

From out of the forest a big black and white snake is rolling down towards our house. It is dangerous.

As Jung showed in his seminar, children's dreams are very often meaningful.[95] Frequently, they refer not only to a momentary emotional event unfolding within the child, but to a future theme of their later life, one that is still hidden deeply within the unconscious. Without wanting to interpret this impressive and frightening dream any further, we can nevertheless recognize that something very special is emerging from within the soul of this child and is approaching it. The dream already gives us an idea of the dimension of its possible significance.

When embarking upon exploring the subject of snakes, one is immediately engulfed by references in myths, fairy tales, legends, spiritual-historical traditions, and all the written documentation of experiences people have had with snakes. As I mentioned earlier, I initially shied away from examining this topic. «How then can I grasp you, endless Nature?»[96] «A snake can have seven thousand meanings,» Jung writes.[97] It was only when I abandoned the inflated notion of wanting to comprehensively address the inexhaustible material on the symbol of the snake that I could even begin! Confining myself to the most important aspects of the snake dreams before me proved to be helpful and useful. This shortcoming will nevertheless underscore the significance of the symbol we are dealing with when we come across it in a dream.

Jung aptly says, «[The snake] appears spontaneously or comes as a surprise; it fascinates; its glance is staring, fixed, unrelated; its blood cold, and it is a stranger to man; it crawls over the sleeper, he finds it in a shoe

95 C. G Jung, *Children's Dreams: Notes from the Seminar Given in 1936–1940.* Included is a child's dream of a snake with shining diamond eyes, and a comprehensive paper by M.-L. von Franz on the symbolism of snakes, p. 240–263.

96 Johann Wolfgang von Goethe, *Faust, Part I,* Verse 455. Transl. A. S. Kline.

97 C. G. Jung, *Dream Analysis (1928–1930),* p. 251.

or in his pocket. […] The snake's presence is frightening; one finds it in unexpected places at unexpected moments. Like the fish, it represents and personifies the dark and unfathomable, the watery deep, the forest, the night, the cave.» Fear of snakes, then, is the fear of all that is inhuman, cold, rigid, dark, abysmal; it is also our "reverent-fear" of the sublime, of all that is beyond the human sphere.[98]

This passage alone gives us an indication of how difficult the topic we are tackling is! Just how arduous it is to understand the snake is revealed in legends in which, for example, a child plays innocently with a snake in secret, or feeds it with milk. When the adults notice what is happening, they are frightened and kill the snake. «But from that day on, the flourishing child began to waste away and soon it died,» one story tells us.[99] Misfortune always follows when parents intervene in this way.

There are many such legends. In ancient mythology, the snake often appears together with a child. There are depictions of a naked child playing among snakes, and nothing happens to it.[100] I would like to include a legend I find particularly charming. It comes from the Bernese Oberland.

«In Willerli, there was a mother and a little girl. And when she took milk from the fire, she put a drop in a 'little mother' – 'ein Mutteli' – (a small bowl) for the little girl who took some on her milk spoon and went outside and said, "I'm bringing the little cat some 'mummy.'" That's what happened. Slowly, her mother began to find it a little strange. While she was working in the 'fire house' – the kitchen – she heard the girl laugh, as if she were playing. She went outside and got a terrible fright. A 'worm' – a snake – was sipping from the little bowl and the girl tapped it on the head with her little spoon and said, "Bread, too!" ("Take some bread, too.") This story was told in Willer. But there was more: when the girl grew up and wanted to marry, the 'worm' came by and dropped a little golden crown into a small bowl for her.»[101]

98 C. G. Jung, *Aion,* [CW 9 II], § 293. On the fish, see also: R. Abt, *Animals and Animal Dreams II, The Fish.*

99 C. Englert-Faye, *Alpensagen*, p. 98. See also the saga of the snake and the child in: M. Sooder, *Zelleni us em Haslita* (record of orally passed down alp sagas), p. 20.

100 M.-L. von Franz, *Puer Aeternus,* p. 82 f.

101 M. Sooder, *Zelleni us em Haslita,* p. 20.

When a child artlessly feeds a snake in a legend, it is often rewarded with a little crown. Less often it is adults who, rather than killing the snake, feed it with milk. This always has a beneficial effect on all of life. The snake's crown brings good fortune, such as grain and money. The crown is sometimes a stone, the snake stone, which has healing properties and can cure, for example, plague, poisoning, or other diseases. It also confers special knowledge, for example, about treasures and how to raise them. When snakes are killed, the child dies, and the people become poor. Gotthilf Isler has written at length on the extremely common motif in legends of the little crowned snake, and its psychological interpretation.[102]

Thus, the little crown has miraculous properties: it brings wealth and well-being, heals diseases, and reveals treasures. It corresponds to the central symbol and goal of the alchemical process, the *lapis philosophorum*, the philosopher's stone, which has exactly those properties. We can gather from legends of the crowned snake that turning toward the serpent – toward one's unconscious 'serpent nature' within – apparently brings rich rewards. Therefore, snake dreams, no matter how uncanny they may seem, always carry the possibility of 'gaining' something, that is, of becoming conscious. When something becomes conscious, when one has an insight about something, or recognizes something, we say that light has fallen upon it – we are enlightened. Hence the snake is also related to the light, as we shall see. Thus, we make note of the sharp contrasts of dark and light, of good and evil, of black and white in legends, a contrast we have already encountered in the dream of the black and white snake.

When the adults kill the snake in this story, they clearly do not understand the child's special connection to the snake. Little children demonstrate this connection all the time: amazed, we can watch how, when they play, little children transform themselves into animals without further ado and converse with living or invented creatures and inanimate objects. They are completely absorbed within their own stories. In these moments, they are in the world of the snake, that is, in the imagery of the unconscious, which poses no threat to them. The adult mind has distanced itself from this realm and can no longer understand it. Indeed, for adults

102 G. Isler, *Lumen Naturae,* "Die Krönleinschlange," p. 154–179.

Fig. 16: Water snake

this area of the unconscious has become, as it were, a meadow in which one could step on invisible, dangerous snakes.[103]

Making a sudden appearance is an essential part of the snake symbol. Psychologically, it corresponds to «psychic happenings or experiences that suddenly dart out of the unconscious and have a frightening or redeeming effect», as Jung puts it.[104] Wandering aimlessly across a meadow, one has no idea that these things might happen. So, when snakes appear in dreams, they indicate a particularly deep level of unconsciousness, according to Jung. Snakes usually appear when consciousness has moved too far away from its instinctual roots.[105] Thus, it seems to me that snake dreams are

103 See examples of snakes as good household spirits in: A. de Gubernatis, *Die Tiere in der indogermanischen Mythologie*, p. 652.

104 C.G. Jung, *Aion,* [CW 9/II], § 291.

105 C.G. Jung, *The Archetypes and the Collective Unconscious,* [CW 9/I], § 282. Ibid., § 282.

extraordinarily difficult to interpret on the personal level. The child's dream above reveals only that the problem of the opposites may have been constellated in this child's life at that time. We shall have to leave it there for the moment and accept that, while snake dreams can sometimes move and impress us, despite our efforts at amplifying them we can rarely assign them to a specific problem as clearly as we would wish.

When snakes or other cold-blooded creatures like dinosaurs or reptiles appear in dreams, they symbolize essential but hidden vital contents and impulses of the unconscious that can block or drain us of our energy. Barbara Hannah, a student of Jung's who was part of a circle close to Jung and a confidante of his for many years, writes: «The snake represents the aspect of the self that manifests, for instance, as an involuntary urge that disturbs all our plans and ideas and that, usually, seems all wrong or, at least, the most terrible nuisance to us.»[106] And: «… for when these depths are touched, only a pretty basic change of attitude is likely to help.»[107]

Let us now try to understand a little of the meaning of snakes in the dreams that follow. The first dream is about an older woman with a teenage grandson. The dream left her perplexed. Was she supposed to do something, or had she perhaps missed something?

Dream 9: The copper-coloured snake

I am with my grandson. We see a long, copper-coloured snake in the bushes. It slithers through the grass near us and bites my grandson's hand. I don't think it's poisonous, but I suck out the poison anyway.

This snake appears to be harmless, but it pays to be cautious, nevertheless. What does the snake want? As in the first dream, it is difficult to recognize its meaning or even if it is a call for action. Perhaps this dream refers to something ahead, something we cannot yet know. The snake is an animal we find difficult to relate to. As a cold-blooded animal, it is too far removed for any emotional connection, like the one we have with a dog, for example. Thus, we struggle to empathize with this symbol.

106 B. Hannah, *The Archetypal Symbolism of Animals,* p. 248.
107 Ibid., p. 165.

The dream is about an adolescent making the transition from being a child into becoming an adult. If, as Jung says, the snake is a part of our instinctual basis, then it represents the world of instincts, including sexuality, which, for a young person in puberty, often appears in a disturbing and dissociating way. The previous unity and spontaneity of the adolescent's personality is disturbed and replaced by a state of insecurity and instability. While this is part of their natural developmental process, it is usually not without its problems, as all parents with pubescent children can testify.

Although this process is natural and desired by the unconscious, it seems to indicate a painful break, for children and adolescents of this age have not yet found their new skin, as it were. Like snakes shedding their skin, adolescents are often unpredictable and aggressive. They are insecure and obnoxious and drive their parents to despair. Grandmothers sometimes have a little more distance to the emotional storms that can affect family life at this difficult time.

The dream says that the snake is copper-coloured, which is perhaps an important detail that could lead us further. The copper-coloured serpent can be equated with the 'copper snake.' There is an idea that has played a major role in Christian culture for centuries that may help us to understand this, namely the idea of the 'fiery' serpent in the 4th book of Moses.[108] During their wanderings, the Israelites fall into a multitude of fiery serpents sent by Jehovah because they had "spoken out against God and Moses." Moses prays for the people, whereupon Jehovah advises Moses to make a bronze (copper) serpent and to place it upon a pole. Whoever looks upon it will not die from snakebite. This gave rise to the idea that in the same way

108 *Holy Bible*, 4th Book of Moses (21, 4-9): «And they journeyed from mount Hor by the way to the Red Sea, to compass the land of Edom: and the soul of the people was much discouraged because of the way. (5) And the people spake against God, and against Moses, Wherefore have ye brought us up out of Egypt to die in the wilderness? For there is no bread, and there is no water; and our soul loatheth this light bread. (6) And Jehovah sent fiery serpents among the people, and they bit the people; and much people of Israel died. (7) And the people came to Moses, and said: We have sinned, because we have spoken against Jehovah, and against thee; pray unto Jehovah, that he take away the serpents from us. And Moses prayed for the people. (8) And Jehovah said unto Moses: Make thee a fiery serpent, and set it upon a standard: and it shall come to pass, that every one that is bitten, when he seeth it, shall live. (9) And Moses made a serpent of brass, and set it upon the standard: and it came to pass, that if a serpent had bitten any man, when he looked unto the serpent of brass, he lived.»

Fig. 17: Pesttaler, Erzgebirge (1528).

that the serpent was placed upon a pole by Moses, Christ was placed upon the cross – Christ as the serpent of salvation. This image can be found well into the Middle Ages. The one serpent was able to keep the many serpents at bay, «Christ is the snake of salvation, the sōtėr snake. […] Christ, so to speak, overcame the autonomous instinctual forces, that is, the evil, and so he is the snake of salvation,» as Jung explains.[109] The copper serpent is the oneness that can calm the multiplicity.

The snake in the dream can therefore be seen as something 'elevated,' a special snake. It is no ordinary snake, but an archetypal symbol. As such, it not only embodies the driven nature of the instincts, but it is also *a symbolic, spiritual creature that is able to unite instinctive processes*. For, as Jung says, there is always the danger that the instinctual processes 'bring us down' and then you are dissolved in the multiplicity.[110] Under certain circumstances, this means that the ego is usually at the

109 C.G. Jung, *Children's Dreams: Children's Dreams: Notes from the Seminar Given in 1936–1940:* «[...] just as Moses exalted the snake on the pole, Christ was exalted on the cross. That's why the Ophites said: Christ is the snake of salvation, the sōtėr snake», p. 217. In the Greco-Roman and East-Asian regions, sōtėr is an epithet (in the sense of saviour, redeemer) for gods and outstanding rulers, but also for Christ (the saviour). Its feminine form is 'sōteira.'

110 Ibid., p. 216.

mercy of oppressive, dissociating fantasies, needs, or compulsions. It seems, however, that these snake processes can be steered into orderly channels by the snake itself.

It is probably no coincidence that the copper-coloured snake in the dream is aimed at the young person's hand, at his conscious 'ability to act,' which is often lost during this difficult time of puberty. It is precisely when important decisions must be made about school and career choices that young people often annoy everyone around them because they 'hang around' lazily and are unable to decide or commit to anything. All their energy seems to have disappeared into the unconscious.

That is why the snake is ambivalent: you do not really know if it is poisonous or not. Copper, when oxidized, produces toxic verdigris. The snake brings consciousness into this unstable, possibly poisonous, state. But that is not all, for it is a copper snake, i.e., a healing snake. This seems to imply that in a symbolic sense it also contains the remedy for the dissociating poison that it itself brings into play. This seems to imply that nature can 'become one' with itself, as it were, i.e., it can balance itself. Therefore, the dreamer may not need to worry too much about her grandson, who, in this difficult situation, is subject to changing moods, thoughts, and fantasies from the unconscious sphere of his instincts.

To suck out the poison from the wound means to absorb it and then to spit it out, i.e., to consciously remove it. I do not know if this is the right solution for the young man in this dream. I suspect that even if you would like to help him, you cannot 'detoxify' this powerful emergence of the instinctual realm in a young person. The dream even says that sucking out the poison is not necessary. Perhaps the dream is telling the dreamer that she does not need to get involved in her grandson's problems. Perhaps some trust in the healing aspect of the copper-coloured 'healing snake' is what is needed! We will come back to this healing aspect of the symbol of the snake later.

As it is our practice in analytical psychology, to understand dreams also on the subjective or inner level of the dreamer, I naturally ask myself what this dream might have meant for this woman. What does the dream depict within the dreamer's own psyche? Was there something resembling a snake, a deeply unconscious impulse, in her psychic make-up that apparently threatened the boy *within her*?

In psychological terms, this boy would represent a spontaneous, individual possibility of inner development. According to the dream, this inner adolescent, like her grandson in puberty, is in a critical, transitional state. The appearance of a snake means there is the danger of consciousness being overwhelmed, of losing its sense of reality. Emotions, unconscious fantasies and impulses, obsessions and delusions can take over, while reason, insight, and control are lost. These are the multitude of fiery serpents. So, for the time being, the dreamer's fear is quite justified.

Because people in earlier times were aware of this danger, they tried to appease the sinister 'serpent powers' through worship.[111] Bronze snakes have been found in the inner sanctum of various temples of the Near East.[112] Snakes were afforded central place in religious cults: they embodied the divine mystery behind not only the dark, impulsive realm, but also behind the highest forms of spirituality and divine wisdom. Any uncertainty about the dangerous nature of the snake in dreams has to do with this ambiguity. When the snake appears, it is always about something essential, even if it is not yet clear whether it is black or white or a mix of the two.

According to the dream, something important, unsettling, and frightening seems to be announcing itself in this woman's unconscious. But it could also mean the beginning of a creative process of renewal or some new spiritual task. Perhaps it is raising the alarm about some creative, spiritual work – as if it were saying, «Pay attention! Don't play at what you are doing, thinking, or writing! This is serious!» It is about 'gnosis,'[113] i.e., about irrational knowledge from inner experience, from the gut, as it were, from your blood, from instinct, a fact of nature, as Jung

111 See A. Schweizer, *Schlangenträume,* p. 140 f.

112 O. Keel: *Das Recht der Bilder gesehen zu werden*, p. 195.

113 C.G. Jung, *Children's Dreams,* l.c. p. 260. See also, ibid. on p. 100, footnote 110: «Gnosticism, from the Greek *gnosis* (knowledge); a belief system that flourished in Hellenistic culture, with a profound influence on Christianity. Gnostics held that the physical world of matter was corrupt and evil, a deterioration of spirit, and that salvation could be attained only through the eternal goodness of the spiritual. Gnosticism was declared a heresy in the fourth century by the Christian Church.» In the German edition of the *Children's Dreams: Kinderträume,* it goes on to say: «In contrast to the purely masculine Christian Trinity, there is place for the dark deity and the feminine within Gnosticism.» (ed.), p. 105, footnote 97. Translated by A. Kappes.

Fig. 18: Snake at the cross. Abraham Eleazar: *Uraltes Chymisches Werk*, Leipzig 1760.

explains. «The Gnostics preach snake wisdom, that is, knowledge *coming from nature itself.*»[114] We know too little about the dreamer to understand what this might mean for her in any detail. My main objective is to provide you with a sense of the depth and meaning of the archetypal symbolism of such a dream. We will come back to the creative aspect of the snake later.

For now, let's return to the subject of the child and the snake. I would like to discuss another dream that mirrors the mythological motif of a child playing with a snake. It was dreamed by a young mother.

Dream 10: The child and the *Boa constrictor*

I am with my son, about 5 years old at the time, in a place in the mountains where I know there are snakes. I tell him he must put his shoes on because of the snakes. He doesn't want to at first, but then he does. Then I see a huge 'boa constrictor' further up, and a child, a boy, playing with the snake. I'm not afraid for the child, but it's still a bit scary for us.

The mother wants her son to wear shoes because he could be bitten by snakes. This is a correct and natural attitude because shoes represent the child's first conscious standpoint towards the unconscious, as it were. It is the mother's task to support this development.

Probably, like all children, her son was still on good terms with the unconscious in a creative, spontaneous way, until the development of his consciousness disrupted his harmony. It is not easy for many mothers to realize that a small child lives largely in the serpentine world of the unconscious, in the world of fairy tales, fantastical ideas, and images. This irrational world of the child involves a lot of creative chaos. It is not the world of rules in which you must tidy up, brush your teeth, and go to school. For the growth of consciousness to take place, however, this paradise in which one plays with snakes must be dismantled. And according to the biblical story of the Garden of Eden, it is at the instigation of the snake that this happens! The shoes enable the child to take its first safe steps out of paradise! We know that children who fail to do this are particularly vulnerable to negative, irrational, complex 'serpent emotions' in their later lives. The original paradise of the unconscious may then

114 Ibid, p. 260.

become a snake pit out of which unpredictable emotions and impulses can erupt at any time.

The dream shows the archetypal constellation in which mother and son now find themselves: both see another child a little higher up playing with a giant boa constrictor. This is the same motif as in the above legend. According to all the mythological parallels, this child is no ordinary child: it is a special, divine child.[115] As we have seen, everything always depends on how the person in question reacts to the situation they find themselves in.

No wonder the young woman in the dream views the archetypal situation of the snake and the child who is playing with it with mixed feelings. After all, the role of consciousness in relation to the unconscious, the snake, is highly uncertain. To what degree may a mother protect her child from the world without spoiling the child and making it unfit for life? How dangerous is it for a child to remain too close to its mother and linger too long in the childhood world of the unconscious? At what point does the snake, the unconscious, become dangerous? Does this happen because the child's original, instinctive way of functioning is disturbed by its growing consciousness? Or because its new conscious awareness is not yet able to separate itself from the unconscious? This question troubles us as adults, too. Are we too close to the unconscious or too far away? Have we lost our bearings by being too alienated from our unconscious instincts, from the realm of irrational emotions and reactions? Or are we too close to them, too much at their mercy, and unable to control ourselves?

The 'divine child' playing with the snake represents an initial paradisiacal state in the psyche. The eternal opposites of the spontaneously instinctive, irrational world of the unconscious and the world of consciousness in which we can realize, name and influence things are not yet opposed to each other. But why does the dream show this image to the young mother?

Perhaps it is drawing her attention to an archetypal process that is beyond her personal responsibility – beyond the worries and concerns that accompany every mother from the first day of her child's life. Perhaps the image is showing her that the snake, the unconscious, has no hostility to the 'divine child' – to the eternally new – or toward the future of the person

115 M.-L. von Franz, *Puer Aeternus*, p. 83.

in question. Her child needs shoes – it needs a firm conscious standpoint to withstand the dangers of the unconscious and the demands of life. This is the task she has been set as the child's mother. With her help, it can learn to find its way in life and its surroundings without having to be at war with the snake. But there is more to it than that.

If we view the dream as a reflection of the events unfolding within the dreamer, then it is about herself, her work, her tasks in the world, about how she copes with life, with her family and her children. But the dream says that behind this, in the unconscious, there is the 'divine child,' the *puer aeternus*, an archetypal symbol that, at bottom, is aimed at bringing forth «a new creative religious attitude and also a renewal of cultural creativity – which can only manifest in a psychological and individual form.»[116] Perhaps that is what this woman needs to know. Perhaps that is the important thing! Her relationship to the unconscious could prove to be crucial not only for her child, but also for herself.[117] This would mean she develops a special closeness to not only the darkest, most eerie, and frightening serpent aspect of the unconscious, but also to the most redeeming, most renewing and creative serpent aspect of the unconscious. People in this situation are not always easy for those around them to understand, and it is not a walk in the park for them either! They have a foot in both worlds, as it were, and may not neglect either! As we have seen, this problem of handling the snake correctly is also portrayed in legends.

In former times in Switzerland, we were not squeamish about snakes. If they were found in the hay or in a wooden bed, "the worm" was beaten to death without further ado. Today, snakes have become rare in most parts of Switzerland. In many legends, as we have discussed, killing a snake brings bad luck. In others, where the snake is spared, a snake queen with a little crown on her head appears and brings wealth and good fortune to the people.[118]

116 M.-L. von Franz, *Puer Aeternus*, p. 274.

117 R. Abt, *Animals and Animal Dreams II. The Fish.* Dream 13: "The Whale Rider,", p. 110–120.

118 See G. Isler, *Lumen Naturae,* chapter "Die Krönleinschlange," p. 154–177. And: H. Hartmann; U. Müller; Ch. Wyss (ed.), *Sagen aus dem Berner Oberland,* p. 35 ff: "Die Schlangenkönigin". And: M. Sooder, *Zelleni us em Haslital,* p. 20.

A cycle of legends relates how someone must kiss a snake in order to redeem someone else to their human form, or to find a treasure. In legends, this rarely meets with success. The snake often gets bigger with every kiss, and the third kiss is almost never dared.[119] According to such mythological statements, it is almost impossible for adult consciousness to approach what is deeply unconscious – the unknown – in the psyche.

The difficulty in approaching the snake and behaving correctly towards it therefore has to do with the fact that the snake corresponds to what is completely unconscious and incapable of consciousness. Jung says: «Its unrelatedness, coldness, and dangerousness express the instinctuality that with ruthless cruelty rides roughshod over all moral and any other human wishes and considerations and is therefore just as terrifying and fascinating in its effects as the sudden glance of a poisonous snake.»[120]

He continues, «The apparition of a snake since the beginning of the world, has been at least very dubious. And as a psychological symbol, it always portrays something deeply unconscious, because it is associated with the intestines and with everything obscure in our psychology.»[121] «As a dream or fairy tale symbol which corresponds to the strongly developed spinal cord system in relation to the head, the snake embodies the work and life of the instinctive, compulsive forces, *the lower centres of our drives and functions that are not subordinate to a regulating consciousness.*»[122] «It is important for psychopathologists to know this, because these contents can produce, at all levels, symptoms that correspond to the physiological functions and are localized accordingly. For instance, the symptoms may be distinctly correlated with the cerebrospinal and the sympathetic nervous system.»[123]

Thus, as I said earlier, snake dreams usually occur as a kind of warning: «Pay attention! Something is approaching from the unconscious psyche, from the realm of instinctive drives or even from the body, which

119 G. Isler, *Lumen Naturae,* chapter "Der Schlangenkuss," p. 98–127 and p. 112.

120 C. G. Jung, *Aion,* [CW 9/II], § 370.

121 C. G. Jung, *The Visions Seminars I*, p. 380.

122 See A. Jaffé, *Bilder und Symbole aus E.T.A. Hoffmanns Märchen 'Der Goldene Topf',* p. 341.

123 C. G. Jung, *Aion,* [CW 9/II], §291.

is particularly far away from consciousness, and which you have no idea about.» Marie-Louise von Franz says that with snake dreams you must even be prepared "that people will act out of the blue."[124] She also points out that what one lacks in consciousness can sometimes exert a kind of secret attraction. You fear it, and at the same time you love it as it is a part of you. This is why the snake in mythology is twofold in nature, black and white, an enemy of the light and at the same time a saviour in animal form.

In legends and fairy tales, the fearsome dragon, like the snake, often guards a precious treasure. In the history of symbolism, the dragon is largely equated with the snake (Greek *dracos* = snake). How should we understand this mythological motif on a psychological level? Jung says that the snake is not only the embodiment of evil and darkness, but that it also seems to possess «a peculiar wisdom of its own and a knowledge that is often felt to be supernatural.»[125] This would be the knowledge of the 'snake of salvation' mentioned above, the precious treasure. For medieval philosophers, this was embodied by the serpent of Mercury, the *serpens mercurialis*. Jung recognized that the serpent of Mercury in alchemy represents the living spirit of the unconscious. We spoke about this earlier when interpreting the dream of the ox-child.

Though they may be difficult to understand, this 'serpent spirit' of the unconscious can convey positive, helpful, expanding, and renewing impulses in dreams. This knowledge often contains the most surprising clues to both personal and collective problems. But the serpentine impulses or serpentine emotions that manifest in dreams can also dangerously overwhelm or even obliterate consciousness. When we interpret dreams, we cautiously try to get a little closer to this ambiguous snake spirit. Caution is required, for it embodies a deep, unapproachable, powerful instinct in the psyche that is completely beyond our conscious control. It is responsible for all kinds of obsessions, including mental illness or even insanity.

That is why there are two snake symbols in alchemy, Marie-Louise von Franz explains. One is the *serpens Mercurius non vulgi*, which is a kind of spiritual soul guide. It embodies the light aspect of the serpent

124 M.-L. von Franz, *Puer Aeternus*, p. 86.
125 C. G. Jung, *Aion,* [CW 9/II], § 370.

Fig. 19: Winged Uräus snake, 20. Dynasty. Valley of the Queens, Tomb of prince Amun-her Chepeschef, a son of Ramses III.

of Mercury. This is the serpentine wisdom of the dream. The other is the ordinary *serpens mercurii*, a chthonic spirit that dwells in matter and primordial chaos. It can be seen as the dark, dangerous side of the unconscious, for example, crazy anima projections, unpredictable and uncontrollable reactions from one's complexes, depressions, compulsions and perversions, terrible fear or impending organic disease. This is the devilish, poisonous aspect of the snake. «There are people who follow the serpent of the unconscious until they end up in an asylum, which means chaos,» says Marie-Louise von Franz.[126] It is vitally important both to know about and to consider these connections when we encounter the symbol of the snake in dreams.

Because the chthonic serpent has to do with the earth, i.e., with the body, with the vegetative nervous system and motor reflexes, it often appears in dreams when we are ill or poisoned. It can be an early symptom

126 See M.-L. von Franz, *Conversations on Aion*, p. 156.

of organic disease, but also of drug or alcohol abuse. From her extensive experience, Marie-Louise von Franz states, «Generally, people who take drugs have quite a lot of snake dreams.» The poisonous snakes in these dreams prompt them to «poison themselves […] because they do not know, or do not see, how to get out of their split in some other way.»[127]

A young girl who suffered from severe anorexia had several important snake dreams within a year, during which she had to be fed several times in hospital. She encountered dangerous snakes in the water, in the lake, or in the pond. She always had to flee. In all these dreams, the snake was dangerous and frightening. This was one of her dreams:

Dream 11: "Cutting up" a snake

I live in a room with my sister. We want to sleep. Dad comes in. I show him the snake. First it 'runs' around Daddy. Then it wraps itself around his hand. Then I say that we have to cut up because we have to eat it.

The strange motif of the snake wrapping itself around her father's hand seems to indicate that her illness has something to do with her father's problem. The dreamer knows that the snake should be 'cut up' and eaten. The motif of dismemberment is an archetypal image of annihilation and renewal. Shamans, medicine men, and sorcerers tell of such dismemberment experiences, which they must endure to fulfil their calling.[128] The ancient Egyptian myth of the dismemberment of Osiris by his brother Seth, who is then reassembled and renewed by his sister Isis, is also well known. In a Sumerian creation myth, the primordial goddess Thiamat is dismembered by Marduk, who creates the world and humans from her limbs. «Life is put together again from the broken pieces,» as Jung explains using many mythological examples.[129]

The 'cutting up' and eating of the snake indicates that the dreamer's problem needs to be assimilated, consciously processed, so that new life

127 M.-L. von Franz, *Puer Aeternus*, p. 88.

128 M. Eliade, *Shamanism: Archaic Techniques of Ecstasy,* p.65. And: M.-L. von Franz, *C. G. Jung. His Myth in Our Time*, p. 99–121.

129 C. G. Jung, *Symbols of Transformation,* [CW 5], § 556.

energy can arise from it.[130] It is the dreamer's own unconscious that is indicating this! I saw this dream as hopeful, but I soon learned that I was probably a little too naive about the dreamer's further development. If we recall how difficult it is to kiss a snake in the legends, we understand how eating a snake must have been an almost impossible task for the dreamer.

In women, the image of their father relates to their animus, i.e., with their own masculine aspect, which is usually shaped by the father, "the first man." In women, animus and snake belong together, as Marie-Louise von Franz says.[131] This represents a problem at the deepest level of the soul, where it is barely accessible. The young girl seems overwhelmed by it. A woman's negative animus can have a strange effect that is difficult to grasp, one which makes the analyst feel emotionally unattached to her. You must always be prepared for some argument to suddenly pop up that will disrupt or even destroy the relationship. I had this very strong feeling about this young woman. Although she appeared to trust me, our relationship was not strong enough to survive a longer period of analysis. More snake dreams came.

Dream 12: The captive snake

We are watching a trapped snake. My arm is very close to it. I want to pull my arm away because it might bite me, but I can't do it. I ask if it doesn't matter if it bites me. The others say it's better if she doesn't bite me. Just then she bites me. It hurts, but it didn't harm me. Afterwards, the snake lies exhausted on the ground.

After the non-poisonous bite, the snake lies exhausted on the ground. It seems to have exhausted itself in reaching the dreamer, as if there was an intention on the part of the unconscious, a kind of energy gradient towards consciousness. Snakes in dreams are often vital contents, such as hidden thoughts or impulses, that force their way out of the unconscious and up

130 C.G. Jung, *Vision Seminars I,* p.276: «So eating the snake in dreams, as well as in fantasies and visions and ceremonials, means assimilation. It is the same idea as eating the body of the Lord in the communion, in order to participate in his strength.»

131 M.-L. von Franz, *Puer Aeternus,* p.86.

to the surface.[132] In this sense, the snake may not be only negative. The very thing that is making the dreamer ill could also foster her healing or help her to become more conscious. The only problem is that the healing aspects of the snake are so far away. They are so deeply unconscious that they can only be brought up into consciousness and understood with great difficulty. In addition, they can often be very frightening.

The ambivalent quality of the snake was reflected in the dreamer's behaviour. She was a difficult person for me to understand. On the one hand she was cooperative, empathetic, and eager to work with me, but on the other hand, by meticulously controlling her weight and stubbornly refusing the intake of any regular food, she appeared to be set upon killing herself. The fact that the snake is in captivity means that it is close to consciousness, from where it can be observed. Perhaps this indicates that she and I have the opportunity to recognize healing impulses from the unconscious in our analytical work together.

The dreamer seems strangely indifferent to possibly being bitten by the snake. She even seems willing to let 'the others,' i.e., collective opinion, decide. Naturally, everyone around her is convinced that she should finally be sensible and just eat. Most often, this sort of advice is utterly pointless. The patient is simply out of her depth, and the lack of understanding from those around her only adds to her isolation.

If the snake is an expression of her illness, this dream seems to reveal a kind of indifference toward it on the part of the dreamer. In truth, the young woman did appear to have little interest in getting well. The problem is rooted in the deepest, serpentine level of her psyche, which would explain why this illness is so difficult to cure and often leads to death. I was shocked at the time to have to watch a pretty, clever schoolmate of one of our daughters slowly starve herself to death in front of everyone, and no one was able to put a stop to this terrible development. It seemed like suicide.

The snake symbol – a life-threatening, autonomous, and completely unconscious symbol – also embodies a secret, inhuman indifference to death. This same dreamer had another dream in which a child in water is devoured by a dangerous snake. She had no idea that something within

132 C. G. Jung, *Dream Analysis. Notes of the seminar given in 1928–30,* p. 646.

her wanted to undo any progress she made. She could not be approached about it either. She wanted to be healed, and she did not want to be healed. This is where the animus comes into play. The dreamer's father was a doctor. Her resistance to all forms of therapy, to hospital stays, and to nutritional programs seemed to have something to do with her father complex. Such a complex can always trigger an animus obsession – a self-destructive dynamic, as was so tragically observed here.[133] We have already addressed this problem in the 'cutting up' of the snake wrapped around the hand of the father.

The child in her dream is her future, her chance to grow and to become an adult, to live her own life. Jung says that often the snake in a young person's dreams simply means a fear of life, but in old age, it means a fear of death.[134] It makes sense that a part of the problem in this instance is an overwhelming fear of life. The dream motif of a child being devoured seemed to me to not be a good sign. In a mythological context, the child-devouring snake is a symbol of death.

In mythology, snakes are also seen as soul animals, as the embodiment of dead souls that appear to the living in this form. This is one aspect of their close relationship with death. Among the San people of Africa, a snake on its back is an annunciation of an impending death. You may not kill it or scare it away. It pays to be afraid and run away, for you now know that someone is dying. "Then we cry," says a San person to W. Bleek, the anthropologist and collector of San folklore in the 1870's.[135] It seems, then, that deep within the psyche where the unconscious merges with the body, as it were, there is an instance that knows one's time of death. It is probably this serpentine unconscious realm that frightens people, but can also provide them with an inkling, or even a certainty, about their imminent death.

It came as a relief to me in my analytical work with this woman to read in Marie-Louise von Franz's work that one often senses a secret mental reservation in people who have been "poisoned by the snake," although

133 M.-L. von Franz, *The Interpretation of Fairy Tales,* "Shadow, Anima, and Animus," p. 114–197. Included are the fairy tales of *King Thrushbeard* and *The Woman Who Became a Spider.*

134 C. G. Jung, *Symbols of Transformation,* [CW 5], § 681.

135 W.H.I. Bleek, L.C. Lloyd, *Specimens of Bushmen Folklore,* p. 431 f.

Fig. 20: Imperial tomb in the cathedral of Würzburg. Wood carving by Tillman Riemenschneider, 16th century.

they are completely unconscious of having such a reservation. It manifests itself in the fact that they «never seem to be completely there. There is always something evasive [about them].»[136] Although I could not put my finger on it, this was exactly what I felt with this woman. The elusive, unapproachable, and potentially deadly serpentine nature of her dreams reflected this. We shall have to leave this dreamer here. Unfortunately, I later lost track of her, and I do not know what became of her.

The next dream addresses the saving, healing aspect of the symbol of the snake in a most impressive way. The dreamer is a young female doctor.

Dream 13: The "redeemer snake"

The intensive care team at the hospital where I work is responding to an emergency to save someone. Both a male and a female colleague are with them: the former is head doctor S., who is calm and experienced, ascetically slim, and the latter is head doctor Sch., who is lively and has curly hair. Their patient is in a cave, and it is unclear what and who they will find there. There is land and water in the cave, and they must swim to their location. In addition to all the medical equipment, they also have a 'medicine' snake with them – at times it is like a wreath in the head doctor's hair, while at other times it swims to the victim, or can be carried like a suitcase. The snake is not a horror: it is part of the team; it is useful, even though I do not know exactly how it heals. Though it is to some extent poisonous, it nevertheless has its place and its job to do.

The victim who is being saved turns out to be a half-dead female corpse. She is a woman aged somewhere between 50 to 70 years, who is dressed in a rather old-fashioned way. Certain signs of death rule out resuscitation, so, contrary to normal procedure, this woman is taken to the intensive care unit for further treatment, where a great effort is made to help her recover. The last image of the dream is of a somewhat distant bustle of work in the intensive care unit.

Fortunately, in this instance, we have some of the dreamer's helpful associations to this dream. They are as follows: «The most striking thing

136 M.-L. von Franz, *Puer Aeternus*, p. 87.

Fig. 21: Mereseger, who loves silence. Goddess of death from Theben.

about the dream for me was that the snake did not terrify me in this dream: I can't remember any other dream in my life in which I did not run away in terror, did not suffer from, or was not frightened by, the sight of a snake. Here it is completely different. The snake is aware of its mission: there is something 'professional' about it. It swims to the scene with a clear task ahead, aware of the difficult situation of the victim, and fully aware of its own powers and skill set. It is a colleague. It is by no means harmless, but it is ready to use its poison 'lege artis.'

It later occurred to me that adrenaline – 1 mg intravenously is the classic drug of every resuscitation – would kill a healthy person, but in resuscitation, it can get the circulation going again. Perhaps it is the same with snake venom: of course, it can kill, but it can also heal.»

If we recall what we said earlier about the symbol of the snake, this dream is self-explanatory! Here the snake is clearly an Aesculapian snake, a snake of healing and redemption, playing its part in a major, almost hopeless, emergency. It is actively cooperating with the doctors, who have all the conscious means of the art of medicine at their disposal. They appear not to be afraid of it. The snake encircles the doctor's head like a wreath, as the crowning glory of female consciousness, as it were. Clearly, this is closely connected with the inspirational aspect of instinct. It can also be carried by a person like a case, as if it were replacing or supplementing the medical bag of doctors – a bag of instinctive knowledge of the unconscious psyche supplementing consciousness. A genuine collaboration between consciousness and the unconscious is clearly being shown here.

It all takes place in a cave and in water. In the dream of the cow's birth (Dream 3), we spoke of the cave's maternal-feminine meaning, and in a subsequent dream (Dream 15) of the three green snakes in the pond, the dream is all about water, one of the most important symbols for the invisible world of the unconscious. This is the world of the snake. In this dream, the snake swims purposefully to the victim and to its place of action. It can therefore be said that where an urgent, largely unconscious, problem is concerned, the instinctual realm – represented by the snake – seems to have a purposeful, higher knowledge. It is both able and willing to collaborate with the conscious mind. If we consider that we usually rely solely on the tangible reality of consciousness to solve our problems, this is an immensely important statement!

This clear dream gives us reason to be extremely hopeful, not only on a personal level, but also in relation to the collective problem of the feminine in our time. The emergency medical team is ready, and the snake is a part of that team. This image reflects an ideal attitude on the part of the conscious mind towards the helpful, although dangerous, impulses of the unconscious. in her associations, the dreamer explains that while under normal circumstances something that is highly poisonous (a dose of adrenaline injected intravenously) can kill a healthy person, in moments of greatest need, it can bring back life. Similarly, medicine from the unconscious can also be harmful if it falls into unqualified hands. Jung was against trying to convince a person to undergo an analysis of the unconscious unless a particularly threatening or otherwise unusual situation required such a dangerous remedy.

This is why, when it came to healing, people always sought the help of a god. Asclepius (Latin: Aesculapius), the Greek god of physicians, is depicted carrying a staff with a snake coiled around it. This image is still present in every pharmacy and most other medical facilities today. According to Jung, this symbol was the original symbol of the sorcerer or medicine man: the staff that turns into a snake and the snake that becomes a magic wand. Jung writes, «The uncanny, inhuman quality of the snake symbolizes the poison that a doctor can handle – it means his secret knowledge, or his hypnotic power. Therefore, a sorcerer was usually accompanied by snakes [...].»[137] [138]

Under normal circumstances, you would never try to bring a half-dead corpse back to life. Nevertheless, the woman in our dream is taken to the intensive care unit for further treatment, and every effort is made to bring her back to life. With the help of the snake, it seems, the impossible is made possible, or at the very least, it is attempted. The problem is recognized and is treated 'intensively' in the hospital, i.e., in the realm of consciousness. The dream emphasizes both the urgency of the situation and the snake's active participation. These are the ideal conditions for a genuine renewal or 'revival' of a lost or forgotten psychic content. An unconditional commitment on the part of the dreamer to such a renewal and an acute awareness of the problem of the feminine is what is essential here.

The corpse or the dying woman who is between 50 to 70 years old could have something to do with a traditional, perhaps bygone, image of the feminine, which, from the middle of the last century, has changed dramatically. Does it need to be 'revived' in a certain sense to counteract our one-sided idea of what a modern woman should be today? The dreamer is not sure whether 'half-dead' things need to be buried

137 C.G. Jung, *The Visions Seminars I,* p.268.

138 J. Narby, *The Cosmic Serpent,* p.34 f. Among the Peruvian Indians, the snake is the mother of the hallucinogenic smoke (ayahuasca), through which the healing effects of plants can be experienced.

Fig. 22: Roman statue of Asclepius, 150 A. C.

for something new to emerge. Could it be that only a part of what the traditional image of women represents will, or must, die or waste away? If the unconscious saw this as meaningful, it could easily represent such an impossible thing.

This dream with its archetypal symbol of the healing snake goes even further. It is undoubtedly referencing the urgent, collective problem of the feminine in our time, a problem that needs to be recognized and needs to undergo 'intensive' treatment. It is not simply a question of people being more sensitive and behaving better: the dream is concerned with the feminine principle of eros, how we all relate to other people, to animals, to nature, to our feeling values.[139] As part of the archetypal structure of the unconscious, this question goes deeper and embraces more. It is about the nature of our individual human relationships, upon which our relationship to the collective is primarily based, as Marie-Louise von Franz points out. Fear, mutual mistrust, insensitivity, and aggressivity among individuals provide the basis for a collective abuse of power, for threats to peace and freedom, and for war. This is why, as Marie-Louise von Franz emphasizes, the problem of eros is of such crucial importance today.[140]

Eros, however, may not be confused with moralism. In recent times, a certain kind of moralistic standpoint – a kind of poisonous dilution of the Christian concept of morality – has been spreading in which all measure is lost. If the feminine quality of eros is a decaying corpse that disappears within the collective unconscious, a tendency arises in consciousness to live out this repressed content in a negative way. What is supposed to be good then leads to all kinds of bad things. Instead of relationship, we see the one-sided condemnation of what is supposedly bad; instead of understanding, there is arrogant intolerance; instead of rapprochement, we witness aggressive confrontation. The collective snake venom of the so-called 'do-gooders' is a perversion of genuine, interpersonal eros.

We can also view this dream of the 'rescue snake' within this larger context. Today, we do not know if the dangerous aspect of the archetypal snake in the collective unconscious is bent on destruction, or

139 See M.-L. von Franz, *C. G. Jung. His Myth in Our Time.* In men, consciousness is generally more committed to the logos aspect of life; in women, this applies more to the eros aspect. p. 70.

140 Ibid., p.145.

Fig. 23: Relief dedicated by Archinos to the oracle god Amphiaraos in Oropos (Attika). In the foreground, the patient dreams of how the god is performing an operation on him; in the background, one can see how the patient is in fact being licked by a snake. Athens, National Museum. 380/370 BC.

if, in the face of our threatened times, it will come to our aid as a rescue snake, as «a healing transformation which might emerge from the depths of the psyche.»[141] The latter will only happen if there is some form of cooperation, as there is in the dream, if enough individuals are aware of the urgency of the situation and view the snake, or the unconscious, as an independent entity. Jung believed we must emphasize the role of the individual to counter-balance the excessive urge towards collectivism in our time.[142] This is undoubtedly as true today as it was then. We see this tendency towards uniformity and standardization in society every day. Politicians and the 'raison d'état' like to call this 'harmonization.'

141 Ibid., p.145.

142 B. Hannah, *C. G. Jung, His Life and Work.* p.335 f.

One might readily ask if it were not better to give up on a patient who is already half a corpse. Or should one work on resuscitating her, even if it seems hopeless? In this dream, the unconscious gives us a clear answer! You must! Despite the great uncertainty that is always associated with the snake symbol, the dreamer says, «The appearance of this healing, helpful force in the form of the medicine snake, the transformation of the horror into a power that serves life, is nevertheless an ongoing treasure for me.» Our modern doctor – this dreamer – like the shamans, both male and female, throughout the ages, can never be sure whether their healing will succeed, whether the result will be renewal or death. Behind the physician's *compassio*, however, is the life-serving power of the snake. Thus, the work in the intensive care unit continues. That is all we, as individuals, can do to revive the principle of eros. The ambivalent symbol of the snake, both dangerous and helpful, is probably the secret behind the dreamer's vocation and the maturation of her personality.

The next dream that was dreamt by a young woman seems to contain a warning. The snakes show a slightly different face here.

Dream 14: Snakes in the house

There are large, whitish, poisonous snakes in the upstairs room of our vacation home or the house in which we live. Someone, possibly a friend, grabs one behind the head and places it in the leaves next to our front door. This is still far too close. I wouldn't mind them if they were a little bit further away, but not in or near our house. The other snakes are still upstairs: they have disappeared behind the boarded wall, but they are still there. This is far too dangerous as they could come out at night when I and the children are asleep and crawl under the blankets for warmth. I'm thinking of calling our neighbour, an old farmer who knows how to handle snakes, to help us.

The dreamer has a sensible attitude toward these snakes. She does not want to kill them; they may stay close to her, but a little further away. And she certainly does not want them in her bed! She sees the snakes as part of nature with their own right to exist, but she must still protect herself from them. Clearly, she needs to be aware of them and keep an eye on them.

Snakes in the bedroom are not the same as snakes in the forest or elsewhere in nature. In contrast to the obscurity of a forest where you must find your way around, the bedroom is both personal and intimate. This is why we understand the forest as the realm of the collective unconscious and the vegetative realm of the psyche, whereas the bedroom, where we can immerse ourselves in the world of dreams, is more the realm of the personal unconscious.[143] Assuming that the snakes come into the bedroom from the forest (because the dreamer's house is in the immediate vicinity of the forest), they get under her skin – they penetrate into her personal unconscious. Jung discusses a similar situation in a seminar[144]. I was amazed that he saw the snakes' proximity as an indication of a good prognosis, which implies she may somehow be able to deal with these snakes. Both the number of snakes and her fear that they might slither into her bed at night emphasize the urgency of the problem: it can no longer be overlooked.

Perhaps the dream is addressing a physical problem of the dreamer. Although, as the dream says, this causes anxiety and dissociation, its origin is still largely hidden. We do not know where the physical problem comes from. It appears and disappears again. The farmer who has both feet on the ground embodies the approach of seeking a sensible, realistic solution. This would mean getting to the bottom of the physical ailment, clarifying it, and drawing the right conclusions. The appearance of the snakes could then ultimately lead to a cure.

The flip side of the disease-causing or poisonous snake is, as we have seen, the snake that brings healing, that brings wisdom from the dark forest, from the earth, from water, all of which are places where we find snakes: in other words, from the unconscious. It is, however, not at all clear which of these two aspects currently has the upper hand in the dream: is it the poisonous or the healing aspect? Which aspect of the mercurial serpent will dominate? The snakes then disappear behind the boarded wall of the room in which the dreamer is sleeping with her children. They are close, all too close, which means that consciousness is aware of the danger

143 On the symbolism of the forest, see: M.-L. von Franz, *The Interpretation of Fairy Tales,* p. 127 f.

144 C. G. Jung, *Children's Dreams,* p. 274 f.

and is, quite rightly, worried. Because of this dream, the dreamer took very concrete measures to deal effectively with her physical problems. She did not want these worrying physical symptoms to disappear once more into the unconscious without the problem having been solved somehow.

If Jungian psychology is sometimes accused of being too little related to the body, dreams like this refute this! Dreams often draw our attention to the fact that something is wrong. They may not tell us exactly what is wrong, which we would naturally like and need to know. They seldom present us with a diagnosis, and what happens within our body unfolds autonomously, unbeknownst to us. For example, we do not know where and why a cancer cell starts to proliferate in our body, and our dreams do not tell us either. In the case of anorexia, however, the snake symbol has provided us with some insight into the nature and severity of the illness. Sometimes the snake seems to be more concerned with the deeper meaning of an illness in the psyche, rather than with the immediate physical symptoms it is causing. What, then, does our dream have to say about this problem?

The whitish colour of the snakes in this dream could indicate a sensory or spiritual aspect. While it is true that these snakes emerge from the lightless depths of the earth, i.e., from the deep realm of the unconscious, their appearance could nevertheless be in the service of healing or of increasing awareness, as it were. In contrast to black which is associated with the earth, with darkness, danger, and the devil, white is associated with light, with brightness, and with spirituality. This is why the white or black/white snake, like the one we encountered in the first dream, also has the above-mentioned spiritual aspect of *mercurius non vulgi*.

On this spiritual aspect of the snake, Marie-Louise von Franz says that our instincts harbour not only instinctive impulsivity, but also a natural wisdom that Jung called 'absolute knowledge' – it is the meaning of instinct, a foreknowledge of the goal.[145] We spoke of this earlier. This spirit, embodied in the image of the whitish snakes, is not aimed at our intellect, at the knowledge of our minds, which we usually refer to as our mental capacity. Rather, it is aimed at permeating our consciousness

145 M.-L. von Franz, *Das Weibliche im Märchen,* p. 246. The fairy tale *The Princess and the Snake* and this quotation are only to be found in the German edition.

and our intellect with its secret wisdom. An uncritical belief in science, for example, is an almost insurmountable stumbling block in the path of the snake. For this reason, especially in science, we often miss out on adopting unconventional, creative approaches that would take us beyond predetermined thought patterns and constricting methods and models. The dreamer was in a phase of her life in which she was looking for new and unconventional approaches in an area that had previously received little attention from science.

Since dreams always allow for many levels and depths of interpretation, the above dream can also be taken as an indication of dissociating, unformed, oppressive ideas and fantasies that can unsettle one's conscious standpoint. Outside demands, experiences, memories, and conflicts can sometimes plunge one into a tormenting treadmill of thoughts, resulting in a sleepless night. According to the dream, in a situation like this, we need to distance ourselves from the incomprehensible and uncanny things that are going on both within us and outside of ourselves. It is sometimes necessary to keep a safe distance from oppressive thoughts, impulses, and moods, for they can become dangerous. They can poison us depriving us of our courage to face life and our future. This sort of situation calls for a healthy, realistic grounding, represented in the dream by the pro-active friend and the farmer, both of whom know how to deal with snakes. It is helpful to sometimes create order in the snake pond, to place things realistically on the ground of reality, thereby removing the obsessive element that robs us of our sleep.

As I said earlier, the whitish snakes in this dream do not suggest only negative aspects: they could also be a signal of something new emerging from the unconscious in a form that, for the time being, is still chaotic. We have already seen that the symbol of the snake embodies all conceivable opposites. We have also mentioned that the snake, like the copper serpent on Moses' staff, is also able to calm the chaotic and to unify it. This makes it a fitting image for the invisible, central instance in the psyche that Jung called the self.

We never know when and how the self will manifest. It usually comes through the door in a manner as unexpected and as frightening as a snake in the grass. Even if we do not react with fear and flight, at the very least, we are unsettled. Many people initially reject the psychology of the unconscious for this reason. They often retreat from the unknown realm of the unconscious with all kinds of rational, pejorative prejudices before they have even interacted with it. This is the archaic human being's primal fear of the unknown, which, despite all our enlightenment, we have still not completely shed. Our fear of snakes lives on!

Alchemy has a thousand names (*mille nomina*) for the self. The most important is the stone, the *lapis philosophorum*, the philosopher's stone. Although regarded as the highest good and the goal of the entire alchemical process, it also shows up as something hostile and dangerous – as a poisonous or fire-breathing dragon or lion, for example. In alchemical language, the dragon/snake «must be killed, or else it kills or devours itself on the principle of Democritus (alchemist): "Nature rejoices in nature, nature rules over nature, and nature conquers nature."»[146] This means banishing with very vivid images the danger that threatens from the unconscious about which the alchemists warned. But, according to this alchemical logion, although this threat emanates from the unconscious, it is also overcome by the unconscious itself, or by the self. As we saw in the dream of the copperhead snake, nature can reestablish its own equilibrium.

Today, on the inner level, we no longer have the options of the past when people killed snakes or drove them away by burning old shoes. Now we know that threatening psychological or organic 'snake symptoms' can ultimately be aimed at healing and expanding consciousness. The poisonous snake of the unconscious can cause the most serious physical and mental illness, but it can also bring about healing. Unlike when we dream of dogs or cats who are close to us and who we can largely understand, dreams of snakes deal with the incomprehensible, which initially fills us with fear, making us defensive. Dealing with these snake impulses is therefore a task that demands the highest levels of patience, perseverance, and all other helpful spiritual powers! Snake dreams can be quite a headache for analysts.

146 Today, our growing interest in alternative methods to complement traditional medicine is just this ancient principle of Democritus being interpreted in a modern way! Many people are increasingly realizing that nature not only brings illnesses, such as viruses and bacteria, but that it also has its own healing possibilities that we can get to know, respect and use. In homeopathy, for example, snake venom or bee venom is successfully used in strong dilutions for healing. See also C. G. Jung, *Alchemical Studies*, (CW 13), § 426, § 430–435.

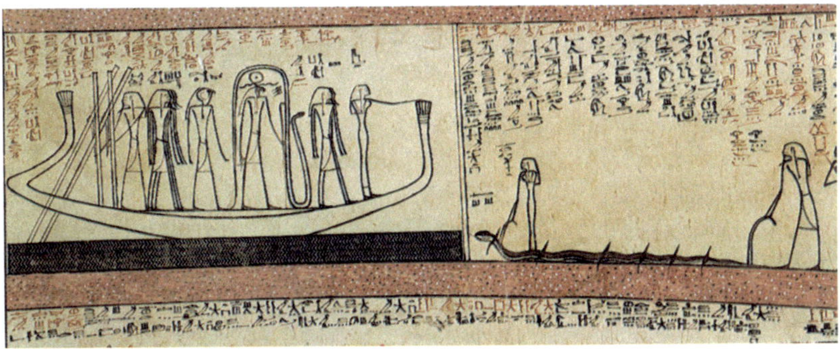

Fig. 24: The Sungod on his night journey, being protected by the Mehen serpent, and the overcoming of the Apophis (Apep) serpent, 7th hour of the Amduat, in the tomb of Thutmose III.

An ancient, historical document from over 3000 years ago which contains snake images deals with the enormous human task of renewing consciousness, or of becoming conscious. This is the Amduat, which means "that which is in the underworld." Painted and written in hieroglyphics, it is a so-called 'underworld book,' initially engraved mainly on the walls of the burial chambers and sarcophagi of Egyptian kings. The oldest known version dates from around 1470 BC, around 3500 years ago. I am basing this on the book by Theodor Abt and Erik Hornung: *Knowledge for the Afterlife. The Egyptian Amduat, a Quest for Immortality.*[147]

The Amduat describes the Sungod's journey in his barque through the night sky of the underworld, his renewal, and finally, his reappearance in the upper world. The evening sunset and morning sunrise of each day inspired the ancient Egyptians to create this magnificent myth of the sun's renewal. This event in the underworld was considered important for the deceased because it explained the eternal cycle of death and renewal – the path to immortality.

147 See the following: Th. Abt; E. Hornung, *Knowledge for the Afterlife. The Egyptian Amduat – A Quest for Immortality*. The book explains the structure, the central motifs of the Amduat, as well as their relation to the reality of the unconscious psyche from a Jungian perspective.

Just how important it was for everyone to know this, including the living, is underscored in the Introduction to the Amduat and later throughout the text: ««Know the way of the Sungod [through the beyond]! – This is a very true remedy, proven a million times.» Or: «It is good to know this [the Amduat, also], for a person on earth, a remedy a million times proven.»[148] The journey is dangerous. There are plenty of snakes in the almost thousand different hostile and friendly beings, gods, goddesses, and animals that accompany the Sungod in the Amduat on his journey. But the journey ultimately leads to the renewal of the Sungod and establishes his immortality.

We now understand the 'underworld' described in the Amduat as the reality of the collective unconscious, which, in shared, typical structures, underlies certain psychic processes common to all people. This journey of the Sungod through the nocturnal underworld describes in images the dangers of the necessary and recurring process of renewal of consciousness from within the dark, nocturnal realm of the unconscious. According to the Amduat, this psychic process of transformation and renewal requires a great deal of knowledge and all kinds of precautions.

A closer look at the role of snakes in this underworld drama will help us to better understand the next dream.

The night journey of the Sungod is divided into twelve hours – from sunset to sunrise. For every hour, there is a description of what is unfolding and why you should know this on the three different levels or registers, whereby the middle register of the first hour is divided. Exposed to all kinds of danger, the Sungod's barque is always at the centre. Apophis (Apep), the giant serpent, presents the greatest danger, capable of derailing the entire process. This equates with the above-mentioned danger of stagnation or flooding by the unconscious, when unconscious contents in the form of violent emotions, unrealistic fantasies, and fixed or morbid ideas take over, so that one's consciousness literally "loses the sun."

There are, however, helpful serpents in the Amduat. In the first hour, beneath the barque of the Sungod is another barque that bears a representation of the Sungod in the form of a scarab beetle. In front of it are three serpents that lead and protect the barque. There are also twelve

148 Ibid., p. 20 (first quote) and p. 9 (second quote).

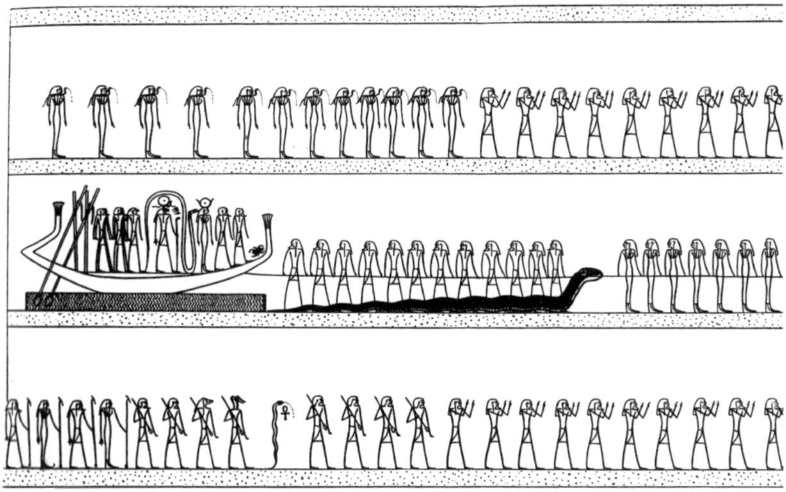

Fig. 25: Regeneration in the serpent of time, 12th hour of the Amduat.

erect, so-called uraeus serpents in the lowest register, who, with their light-bringing breath, illuminate the darkness of the underworld ["who brighten the darkness of the netherworld"]. They also perform the task of protecting the Sungod and the dead, for whom the Amduat shows the path to immortality and renewal. Serpents are depicted everywhere in the Amduat, not least at the transitions from one hour to the next, where the danger of the procedure failing is at its greatest. Although depicted as hostile even in the seventh hour, in the twelfth and final hour Apophis and the danger he represents is averted. In this twelfth hour, the largest serpent is no longer hostile to the Sungod, but moves in the same direction as him, helping him. It has become a helper and a bringer of renewal, not only of the Sungod, but also of all the other deities who accompany the Sungod on his journey. From now on, the latter not only carries the sun disk on his head, but also the erect uraeus serpent. Twelve male and thirteen female goddesses now pull the sun barque through the body of the great serpent, an image of the final renewal and transformation of the Sungod.

In psychological terms, this ancient myth speaks of the healing properties of the unconscious and its ability to renew consciousness.[149] The dreams people dream today are still about this.[150]

We must be content with these few, unfortunately all too fragmentary, remarks on the meaning of the snakes in the Amduat. They will nevertheless be of use to us when we move on to the next dream. It comes from a married mother of two small children who had fallen in love with a much older man who was also in a long-term relationship. For outer reasons, the relationship turned out to be difficult, almost hopeless.

Dream 15: The green snakes in the pond

Walking in the forest with my children, I come across a 'bright,' white forest pond. A pebble path leads past this pond. My two girls are playing on the bank when suddenly three dark green snakes with white tongues swim towards us (coming out of the pond). They are aggressive and want to bite us. Their tongues are bright. We run to the path and manage to save ourselves from them. We were not bitten.

Like the forest, where water and dark, earthy, vegetative life predominate, the pond is an image of the unconscious. All life is based on water and the vegetative rhythm of life. Emerging out of this very deep, ancient psychic layer are three dark green snakes. The dreamer's unconscious has come to life; something is on the move.

We associate green with poison and toxins, for example, but green is also the colour of nature, natural life and therefore, of hope. «In the Middle Ages, green was considered to be the colour of the Holy Spirit, of life, procreation and resurrection.»[151] Green is also part of numerous vegetation and fertility customs concerned with death and renewal. On Maundy Thursday (in German, 'Gründonnerstag' or Green Thursday), there is a rich

149 See Th. Abt, *Knowledge for the Afterlife. The Egyptian Amduat – A Quest for Immortality.* And: E. Hornung, "Söhne der Erde – Schlangen im Diesseits und Jenseits der Ägypter". In: E. Hornung; A. Schweizer, *Die Weisheit der Schlange.*

150 See also Sabine Abt, *Der Flammenhimmel. Die Geschichte einer wunderbaren Reise.* This story begins with the terrifying appearance of a destructive black snake and ends with its miraculous transformation.

151 M.-L. von Franz, *On Dreams and Death,* p. 24.

Fig. 26: Hecate Triformis. Paris, Bibliothèque Nationale.

tradition focused on warding off illness and maintaining health and fertility. On this day, among other things green herbs and vegetables are eaten.[152] In alchemy, *benedicta viriditas* (blessed green) is «like a hidden spring, where young, green seeds sprout from seemingly dry soil, promising a future harvest.» This 'green' of the alchemists suggests poisonous verdigris, for example, but also «the secret indwelling of the divine spirit of life in all things.»[153] Green could therefore indicate both danger and hope, in the sense of natural growth and the future. Thus, the green snakes have to do with the deeply unconscious principle of both life and death.

That there are three snakes is no coincidence. In this context, it is reminiscent of the already-mentioned widespread idea of the three goddesses of nature who determine the fate of human beings. In the Germanic world, for example, these are the three goddesses of fate, the Norns, while in the Celtic world there is the three-times depicted Brigit; there are the three Greek Moirs, and many moon goddesses are depicted in threes. There is also the Greek underworld goddess *Hecate triformis*, the mistress of birth and death with three heads or faces.[154] The three snakes therefore have to do with the fateful passage of time and the inexorable, unilateral movement of life that no one can escape.[155]

In mythical representations of the past, the snake is closely related to time. Time itself was originally represented as a serpent, for instance carrying zodiacal signs upon his back.[156] Time can be seen as a constant stream that flows from the past into the present and from the present into the future. It was also perceived as an eternal circling: years, months, days arrive and are swallowed up by the snake of time, only to periodically return. This is also an aspect of the famous symbol of the dragon or the serpent, the *Ouroboros*, that chases its own tail.[157]

152 E. Hoffman-Krayer; H. Bächtold-Stäubli, *Handwörterbuch des deutschen Aberglaubens,* Bd. III, 1186–1196.

153 C.G. Jung, *Mysterium coniunctionis,* [CW 14], chapter "Adam and Eve," § 289.

154 *Lexikon der germanischen und römischen Mythologie I*, 2, 1885.

155 M.-L. von Franz, *Interpretation of Fairy Tales*, p. 90.

156 C.G. Jung, *Children's Dreams,* p. 205. See also: Th. Abt; E. Hornung: *Knowledge for the Afterlife. The Egyptian Amduat – A Quest for Immortality.*

157 C.G. Jung, *Dream Symbols of the Individuation Process,* p. 90. See also *The Visions Seminars II*, p. 1042: Aion, the Mithraic god of time, entwined by the serpent.

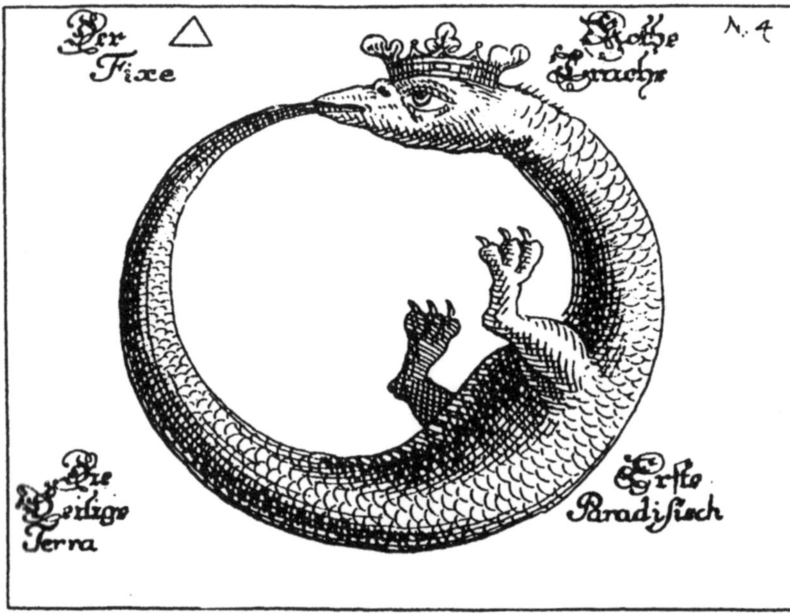

Fig. 27: Ouroboros. Abraham Eleazar: *Uraltes Chymisches Werck*, Erfurt 1735.

If we now consider this important aspect of time that is tied to the symbol of the snake, then this dream could be about a profound, spiritual process of change as it unfolds in time: it is not a straight, fast road, but a winding snake path.[158] In view of this, the dreamer's love story would not then be a superficial love story, but rather, with careful observation of her dreams, a slow discovery of what the serpent nature goddesses might have in mind.

The three snakes, which we associate with the three goddesses of nature and fate, seem to be saying: «Watch out! For better or for worse, what happens to you has to do with fate, with the fateful course of your life, with your deepest, feminine-maternal nature.» Fate also includes the ruthlessness of nature, which makes no distinction between eating

158 C. G. Jung, *Deutsches Seminar. 5.–10. Oct. 1931*. «If we think we are now going left, the snake knows we are only turning left to go to the right. All nature reaches its destination by the crooked path; it is insultingly illogical.» Translation A. Kappes.

and being eaten, between living and dying. No one knows whether the future will bring a cruel or a kind fate. The dreamer flees in horror with her children from the snakes, which, I suppose, it is reasonable to imagine we all might do.

Strangely, these eerie snakes have white tongues. A snake's tongue is used to detect odours on the ground, which is why they frequently flash out of their closed mouths. In truth, one hardly ever sees a snake's tongue, and certainly not from a distance. The tongues of the "dream snakes," which are apparently clearly visible, are more reminiscent of a human tongue, with which they could speak if they were human. This is a detail we need to pay attention to. It could indicate an inherent possibility on the part of the unconscious to communicate. This is, of course, only an assumption which may or may not be confirmed by further amplification.

Does the colour white mean anything to us in this context? In the last dream about the whitish snakes in the bedroom, we spoke of the *mercurius non vulgi*, the spiritual, illuminating aspect of the unconscious. As light or as the colour of transition from one state into a further and new state, the colour of white is positive. We are familiar with this: the clothing of a person being baptized is white, along with many other rites of passage in which the initiate wears white clothing as a sign of undergoing transformation and renewal. In popular belief, white snakes are always special snakes that know the secret path, that bring wisdom and revelation, that know about the secret treasure, etc.[159] They are helpful animals. White is the colour of their enlightenment. But white can also mean "without life," in the sense of winter's cold, snow, and ice.[160]

These three snakes with their white tongues thereby embody all the possibilities of psychic expression – good and evil, helpful and dangerous – and the dreamer is right to be afraid of them. The unusual, whitish colour of the forest pond where her children innocently and fearlessly play could indicate a lightening of the natural darkness of the unconscious. This might lead us to view the white tongues of the snakes in a positive way, like the twelve cobras of Amduat which breathe fire and light and thus illuminate the underworld. These white tongues could represent a kind of

159 C. G. Jung, *Children's Dreams,* p. 215 f.

160 Th. Abt, *Introduction to Picture Interpretation,* p. 107.

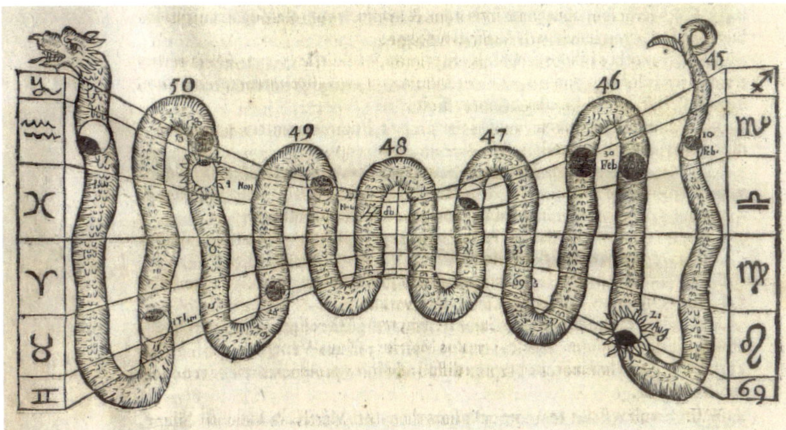

Fig. 28: The snake of time. Table for calculating solar and lunar eclipses. According to ancient legends, these were brought about by a dragon devouring the celestial bodies and spitting them out again. Athanasius Kircher: *Ars magna lucis.* Amsterdam 1671.

almost human-like expression of some higher wisdom of nature arising out of the dreamer's seemingly unsolvable life and love problem.

Nevertheless, we must take the dream as a warning because it is not clear what is emerging from the dreamer's unconscious which may or may not prove to be threatening to herself and her children. While their green aspect may indicate a hopeful renewal of life, their snake aspect could also indicate a constellation of her instinctual nature, for example, her sexuality. The pressure the dreamer feels in her seemingly hopeless life situation could escalate into panic and short-sighted action (snakes readily trigger panic), which could break up her family and cause unforeseeable damage. But right now, the dreamer manages to get herself and her children to safety. This gives one hope that a fear-induced distance from emotional events will not allow her difficult situation to get out of hand!

As a symbol of renewal, the three snakes could also point to the potential of inner, spiritual development and renewal from within the depths of her feminine personality. Ultimately, for a woman, this always means a confrontation with the animus, with her unconscious, masculine aspect. It seems no coincidence that the unconscious has manoeuvred the dreamer into such a difficult, unconventional love story. Our consciousness is apparently 'made' in such a way that no real change is possible without pain. The cruel initiation rites of archaic peoples are a quite concrete demonstration of this psychological fact.

As explained earlier, when we are dealing with an archetypal dream, we must largely refrain from pursuing the personal thread of the dreamer's life, and the question of whether she succeeded in taking up the confrontation with the animus and resolving her love problem. However, the motif of the three green snakes in the forest pond reveals how deeply such an experience of love can lead one into the depths of one's unconscious psyche, and this should by no means be taken lightly, for where there are snakes, there is danger at hand.

The next dream is a dream I had many years ago when I was preparing a lecture. Of course, I had the usual concerns that I would not be up to the task. Surprisingly, the snake had something to say about that.

Dream 16: The rattlesnake entwined around the leg

I must give a lecture. Somehow outside in an open field. I firstly remove from the lectern all the books and papers that are blocking my view of the audience. I ask the people sitting further away to come closer.

Now I walk to this lecture over a rocky hill in a desert-like landscape. I have my old female dog with me who can't walk up steep hills very well. A young woman stands next to me to help the dog. Then I realize that I am wearing a small rattlesnake around my leg, like a ring. I trust that it knows me and won't bite. Will people fear it? I think only if something were to happen, a bang or a clap of thunder or something similar, then the snake would get scared and bite. That would be the end.

The dream seems to refer to a spiritual or creative problem, for the lecture is about imparting spiritual knowledge. My relationship to the people who will be listening to me is important. Too many books and papers – too much theoretical knowledge – could disturb this relationship by making the whole thing boring!

Working at one's desk, writing and correcting, organizing and combining theoretical knowledge with one's own thoughts, can sometimes literally lead one into the desert. My dog, the embodiment of eros, the relationship that connects and inspires me and my audience, is having difficulty running along at my side. Not a good situation! The desert is hardly a place of creativity. In a desert, you are exposed to many dangers: scary animals that lie hidden in the sand can suddenly appear and cause you to stumble. The desert comes to life. As a dream image, it always represents a situation of loneliness, where an inner state can suddenly impose itself in the form of strange or oppressive thoughts and images, or where a process does not flow because there is no water. Fortunately, a young woman is there, a helpful shadow figure who apparently has even more energy and strength at her disposal than I do; I could easily have felt desperate. In this 'parched' situation, a snake appears, coiled around my leg.

I clearly realize that this snake is not hostile toward me. It is wrapped around my leg like a ring, but it does not wind its way up; it does not threaten me. Why am I dreaming this strange image? Two symbolic circles are being combined here: the snake and the ring. They belong together and yet each must be considered separately. From a psychological point of view, we can say that the snake as a circle or ring is a symbol of the self. But which aspects of the self are addressed by this? Right now, we only know that, in accordance with its ambivalent nature which we discussed earlier, the snake is either dangerous or helpful.

Let's see if we can get closer by considering the symbolism of the ring. Ring processions, ring walls, ring dances, the magical rings, and circles of sorcerers to summon spirits, etc., all originally had the function of marking off a protected area from the outside world. We find this not only in mythology but also in countless folk customs, for example, in the alpine blessing of some mountain peasants who, in certain places, still place a protective ring around the alp in their evening prayer for themselves and their cattle.[161] Such a ring is a symbol of magical protection against the surrounding chaos of the unknown, the hostile earth and other spirits, against all that is dark – against the unconscious.

161 See E. Renner, *Goldener Ring über Uri*.

Let's now consider the snake as a ring. The snake is a symbol of the deepest, most unconscious instinctual world that can become dangerous for us. The ring, on the other hand, symbolizes a form of magical protection of ego-consciousness against the superior knowledge of this unconscious instinctual world.[162] Encircling my leg, it is as if it were saying, «You can't get away from me. You are bound to me. I am your threat and your protection.» I find myself in a delicate situation in the desert. It is well known that evil spirits and demons also live in the desert. In Islam, these are the jinn, who can frighten people and lead them astray. The desert is also the place where people can easily die of thirst or starvation. If the ring were negative, it could mean that a person is trapped in a complex, in their emotions, or in a vicious circle.[163]

In psychological terms, such a dream image depicts a situation in which the conscious mind is cut off from the water of life, as it were, which energizes the unconscious. Then, like the evil spirits of the desert, negative thoughts and fantasies can emerge. In such an emotionally charged situation, a magical snake ring can protect one's conscious mind from the forces of the unconscious. A calming 'concentration' on one's own centre, i.e. on the self, becomes possible. A quiet confidence that things will work out, that it is possible to present the material in a non-superficial way, can then emerge. This would be a self-confidence that is based on the helpful aspect of the unconscious, rather than on the intellect. Then one feels somehow carried, even if one is sitting in the desert.

But, the dream says, if a bang or thunderclap were to happen, the ring of the snake could become dangerous: it could bite, and that would be the end. This makes sense, because the proximity to the snake, i.e., to the unconscious, always harbours the danger that violent 'snake emotions' could erupt and poison everything.

In his Visions seminars, Jung talks about how the union of the divine (because this is what the overpowering forces of the unconscious

162 C. G. Jung, *Dream Symbols of the Individuation Process,* p.87 f. See also this double aspect in the therapeutic principle of homeopathy: *Similia similibus curantur* (like is cured by like.) To treat illnesses, medicines are used in high dilutions that would cause certain symptoms in healthy people in higher doses. However, it is precisely these 'similar' symptoms that they can cure in a sick person.

163 M.-L. von Franz, *Interpretation of Fairy Tales,* p. 82.

were originally perceived as) with the human always requires 'keeping still.' In the mysteries of Eleusis, which involved receiving the god in the form of a snake, the initiate even had to kiss the divine snake – the same motif as in our legends, mentioned earlier. This was, of course, both repulsive and terrifying, and you were not allowed to panic. Thus, we may not identify with these snake emotions:[164] to do so would mean losing our centred and concentrated connection with the unconscious. We would inevitably become entangled in superficiality and our complexes. When emotions take over on a collective level, revolutions and wars are just around the corner.

While I was writing this chapter, I received an unpleasant phone call that turned into a nasty argument! That was the end of keeping quiet! It was also the end of writing, and the end of my creative phase: I was completely poisoned and had to spend two days calming down both the snake and myself before I was able to concentrate again!

Even if you engage with the creative spirit of the unconscious in your work, you can still find yourself suddenly out of step. Your conscious plans no longer lead to the goal. You lose your bearings, as if in a desert, and you do not know how to get out of this state! Anyone who struggles with creative work can tell you a thing or two about this. The work of artists, poets, musicians, etc. does not fall into their laps: it usually involves some desert-like emptiness in which nothing works! Wherever the serpentine spirit of the unconscious is constellated, it may or may not come out well. The most important thing at this moment seems to be not to panic! The serpent may then bring about a completely unexpected solution, something that we could not have thought of. Barbara Hannah writes. «When a serpent appears in a dream or active imagination, he often represents the utterly unexpected solution, something we could never think of consciously in a thousand years.»[165]

Perhaps, then, the dream of the rattlesnake compensates my attitude that underestimated the foundation of creativity, namely, the spirit of the unconscious or the wisdom of one's own inner nature, which the snake also represents. When in the 'desert state,' you often devalue yourself.

164 C. G. Jung, *The Visions Seminars I. Notes of the Seminar given in 1939–1934,* p. 603.

165 B. Hannah, *The Archetypal Symbolism of Animals,* p. 225.

Perhaps you are annoyed by your lack of intellectual insight or talent as an orator, or some other superficiality – like whether your clothes and shoes match! Then you are insecure and susceptible to criticism and may easily panic. It could all go wrong after all. Panic prompts the snake to bite. In other words, when unconscious emotion gets the upper hand, it poisons and spoils all that is constructive.

Fear and panic make us lose our heads. Stoking fear is an effective way for politicians around the world to shut down people's reason and spread emotions, which are then easily channelled into entrenched beliefs and ideological battle zones. Everything becomes toxic and dangerous. This is how wars break out, even though nobody wants them. Panic evokes the dangerous side of the snake. A false attitude on the part of consciousness provokes the chthonic serpent spirit of the unconscious in its darkest, deadliest form.

Earlier, we spoke about the earthy aspect of the snake that has to do with insects, reptiles, and invertebrates, with a very old form of life, with the ancient layers of the nervous system and our deepest physical reactions. But now we are discussing the serpent spirit of the unconscious. For us, spirit seems to be something that has more to do with what is above us: spirits in the air, the mind, our imagination, thinking, or intellect. We have already touched upon this subject. So again, we ask: What is this all about?

The concept of there being a spirit of the unconscious has to do with the development of consciousness. Rather than simply falling from the sky, this development begins with the physiological. It is based, as it were, in the body's unconscious. Consciousness arises from the unconscious. In our «hereditary mass, we consist, on the one hand of a natural being of primitive instinctuality, on the other hand of a spiritual hereditary mass.» This sets limits on our instincts, as we discussed earlier. This 'spiritual inheritance' contains the dynamic, symbol-forming spirit of the unconscious, which creates new "ideas, artistic inspirations and constructive hunches and fantasies" in individuals, which are then sometimes adopted and imitated by the group that surrounds the individual.[166]

166 M.-L. von Franz, *C. G. Jung. His Myth in Our Time,* p. 90.

An image of this dynamic of the unconscious mind towards consciousness is the Hindu symbolic representation of the Kundalini serpent, a coiled snake deep within the lowest part of the human body that crawls up the spinal cord and strives for the light of wisdom. But in our culture, our typically Western overvaluation of the mind in the form of rationality and intellect means that snakes in dreams often move in precisely in the opposite direction: they go down into the depths. Where primarily rational concepts, statistical thinking, logic, efficiency, predictability etc. drive dynamic development, the snake appears as a compensatory warning call of our neglected instincts. We might experience this as a kind of 'gut feeling,' for example, which could offer something other – a complementary perspective – to our conscious approach.

Gut feelings rarely have a clear direction. At first, they unsettle us for they clash with our conscious viewpoint or call it into question. We do not really know what the snake wants. A snake, however, never crawls in a straight line: it moves along with "serpentine movements." A symbolic snake path, then, is a winding path – a tedious, lengthy path that only leads to the goal via seeming detours. This is the winding path mentioned above. It is often strange and somewhat scary to us because we cannot assess it in advance, because it always seems to lead us the wrong way, and because it is beyond our control. But, in certain circumstances, Jung tells us, this is the form in which psychic energy can flow. *The snake is the symbol for the wisdom or spirit of nature: its serpentine movement is simultaneously both the detour and the shortest way to the goal.*[167] But from the perspective of the individual, the serpentine path always appears to take fateful detours and aberrations. It «is a *'longissima via,'* not straight but snakelike, a path that unites the opposites [...] a path whose labyrinthine twists and turns are not lacking in terrors,» Jung explains.[168]

In an era in which we are constantly stumbling along behind some new threat, trying to come up with seemingly new solutions, it would seem we are also urgently in need of some helpful serpent wisdom for both society and politics. With the help of the serpent spirit, we could hope to somehow be able to counter the devilish aspect of the serpent, for example

167 C.G. Jung, *The Visions Seminars I,* p. 510.

168 C.G. Jung, *Psychology and Alchemy* [CW 12], § 6.

the danger from the collective unconscious that is currently threatening the world. This wisdom, however, never manifests in the mainstream, but rather in the very unconventional, creative ideas and proposed solutions of individuals who do not conform to the zeitgeist. Behind the rejection, demonization, and modern *annulment* of everything that does not fit into current, collective ideas of our time is the fear or terror of this unconventional serpent spirit of the unconscious.

On a personal level, we often struggle with a problem that does not seem to be solvable for a long time. It is then sometimes advisable to simply let go, to hold back our anger or frustration, and to endure the fact that the problem could get worse by doing nothing. By enduring our fear, our anxiety, our sorrow, our depression, by enduring the fact that we don't know what to aim at, or what a solution might look like, we provide the unconscious – the snake – with the opportunity to intervene. The redeeming idea can then suddenly appear, and we are back on track. There is no need to pat ourselves on the back for this, for it was the snake's doing! Our efforts, our sometimes desperate struggle for understanding, for the right expression, for the right way of behaving, has activated this deep level of the psyche. The dream image of the rattlesnake coiled around my leg seems to express something of this.

One important aspect of the snake must be mentioned here. Because snakes grow, they must repeatedly shed their old skin. Underneath, a new, wonderfully shiny, colourful skin is revealed. Snakes shed their skin regularly, approximately every month, until they are five years old. With each molt, they renew and transform themselves, a process that has undoubtedly fascinated people from time immemorial. Because of their constant renewal, people even imagined that snakes were immortal. The snake thus became a symbol of constant transformation and renewal, a symbol of the path that leads through the mysteries that bring about transformation. This is reminiscent of the serpents in the *ancient Egyptian Amduat*, the text that describes a process of transformation and renewal.

In ancient times, there were many so-called 'incubation sites' of Asclepius and other healing gods. At the birthplace of Asclepius, the main sanctuary of Epidaurus, there was a labyrinth with a snake pond in the middle. It was believed that the god they worshipped manifested himself in these snakes. Sick people and those seeking help turned to him by spending the night in a kind of cell in the sanctuary near the snakes, hoping for helpful dreams. These were interpreted by priests and doctors, who also took their own dreams into account.[169] By not simply imposing a psychological theory on our patients, but by trying instead to follow the clues of the unconscious in their dreams, no matter how uncanny and difficult they may be to understand, we, as therapists, are basically doing the same thing today!

The ancient philosophers eventually formulated the idea of a "soul-guide," – in Greek, a 'psychopompos' – in the form of a guiding serpent.[170] From this, the Christian Gnostics developed the image of a redeeming serpent, which, as we have seen above, was identified with Christ. As already mentioned, the serpent was a well-known allegory of Christ in the Middle Ages. It was attributed the gifts of wisdom and supreme spirituality.[171] In medieval depictions, instead of the crucified Christ, it is often the snake that hangs on the Cross. Like the crucified man, the snake hangs there in its own light-dark contrasts, uniting them at the same time.[172]

As the image of the crucified serpent would take us deep into Christian and Gnostic symbolism, this is where we shall leave this dream. However, as we move on to the next dream, let us bear in mind the theme of transformation and the image of the redeeming snake. The next dream was dreamt by a young man. The widespread theme of being entwined by a snake reappears here.

Dream 17: A viper (common European viper) winds its way around me

Somehow, I reach a hilly area, an area that is almost overgrown. There I sit down in the tall, dry grass. It is early spring. Further up the rather steep hill, a female sits under a large, green deciduous tree. From

169 M.-L. von Franz, *C. G. Jung. His Myth in Our Time,* p. 110 f.

170 C. G. Jung, *Dream Symbols of the Individuation Process,* p. 290.

171 C. G. Jung, *Aion,* [CW 9 II], § 369 f.

172 Vergl. R. Abt, "The Tree", In: R. Abt, I. Bosch, V. Mackrell, *Dream Child,* Dream no. 45 of a modern woman with the motif of a cross entwined with a snake, p. 152. And: R. Abt, "The Cross". In: *The Saint and the Pig*. p. 149–168.

there, and in some way because of our contact, a snake comes shooting towards me, like an arrow, and begins to wrap itself around my body. At first, I am terrified, as I can see that it is a cross adder. But I know that I must stay calm because the animal has no malicious intent. No, the snake writhes and turns around and around, in an almost loving way. I become more and more familiar with the situation. Then the animal disappears again. Now I must go back down the mountain to the people. I know that I have had an experience that I cannot share. Now I know that there is a great danger within this neglected nature for those who cannot deal with it. I return to a group of people who are doing gymnastics. As I have no gym kit with me, I can join in the gymnastics in my underpants.

In this dream, there are three of the most important archetypal symbols: the tree, the woman, and the snake. They emerge, as it were, from the darkness of the unconscious where all archetypal images are somehow contaminated with each other or overlap, making it «possible to establish associations of meaning and motif, even of identity, between *every* archetypal symbol and every other one,» as Marie-Louise von Franz explains.[173] Generations of researchers and collectors have recorded customs and traditions in this way and explained them from their respective points of view without ever looking at the people behind them. This has, of course, provided psychology with valuable material for understanding dream symbolism, which is why we study customs, fairy tales, myths, and medieval philosophy.

However, because an archetypal symbol brings up the entire unconscious associated with it, so to speak, you can get completely lost in the interpretation of a dream. Everything leads to everything else. Snake, woman, and tree can then be amplified at will with water, child, sun, forest, stone and so on. The material always offers further connections of meaning.[174] The mythological associations get out of hand; the speaker's papers pile up as in the dream above, and the audience falls asleep. This is why we must take feelings into account in our interpretation. Does an

173 M.-L. von Franz, *C.G. Jung. His Myth in Our Time,* p. 129. From p. 125–130, M.-L. von Franz gives an excellent, summarized explanation of the theory of archetypes.

174 See M.-L. von Franz, *Interpretation of Fairy Tales,* p. 14 f.

Fig. 29: Uraeus snake with cow horns, 19. Dynasty. Valley of the Queens, tomb of Nefertari.

interpretation make sense to us, are we satisfied with it, or have we lost our way in the archetypal labyrinth of amplifications? Only after considering them can we profitably consult Jung's works, such as *Aion* or *Symbols of Transformation*, without being overwhelmed by the wealth of material presented there.

If we now try to get a little closer to the meaning of the dream, we naturally do not know where this will lead us, and that is a good thing. A quick, off-the-cuff interpretation would undoubtedly not do justice to the depth and complexity of a dream like this! First, let's look at the tree as a symbol, then at its connection with the feminine, with the woman in the dream, and finally, let's look at the snake, which is linked to both.

Old trees still impress us today, and many people put up a fierce fight whenever yet another old tree must make way for some building project. For the ancients, large trees were objects of cult worship. It was the Christian missionaries who first felled the huge, sacred trees of the Germanic tribes.[175] They did so in the belief that by doing so, they would eradicate pagan idolatry. Despite this violent Christianization which cut the Nordic peoples off from their spiritual roots, as it were, the tree retained its significance within the psyche.

That trees are rooted in the earth yet seem to touch the sky with their branches is central to our understanding of them. They have always been perceived as a way of connecting what is below to what is above, which is why we have ideas such as the tree of life, the tree in the Garden of Eden, the shamanic tree, or even the idea of a world tree or a world axis. According to the Edda, the great Icelandic creation epic, the roots of Iggdrasil, the Germanic world tree, are embedded within the depths of the world of the dead and in the ancestral past, while its branches reach up to the heavens.

Today, we see the growth of the tree from the earth towards the sky with all its associated meanings as a symbol of a human being growing from their unconscious roots, from their inner nature. This happens according to the pattern set within them, in the same way that an apple

175 J. Brosse, *Mythologie der Bäume,* p. 273. And: R. Abt, "The Tree". In: R. Abt, I. Bosch, V. Mackrell, *Dream Child,* p. 141.

tree can ever only become an apple tree, or an oak tree, an oak tree, and so on. A tree's growth process into its final form is ultimately an image of the individuation process – the process of spiritual growth of the human being realizing the possibilities inherent in them, according to Jung.[176] Like the slow growth of a tree, our development takes place over a lifetime. We sometimes sense this in certain people who seem to have a special charisma and effect upon those around them. This has nothing to do with their being smarter or more successful than others, but more because, like a tree, they have managed to weather the storms of life while holding space for their inner growth process to unfold.

Another aspect of the tree has to do with timelessness and transformation, with death and rebirth, which take place continuously in nature. A deciduous tree seems to die every winter, but in spring it flourishes anew. It is constantly changing and renewing itself throughout the course of the year. At the same time, it is entirely rooted in the earth and cannot move away. Unlike humans, it has no way of escaping the laws of the earth. In contrast to animals, we human beings within our artificial world and with our different pace of life, seem to have freed ourselves from being earth-bound and from the laws of nature, says Jung.[177] But of course, these natural laws have not disappeared from the reality of the soul; they have merely been 'gilded,' neglected, and underestimated. At bottom, this is the problem that the dream is dealing with.

When I was working on a summary of the significance of the tree many years ago which I presented to Marie-Louise von Franz, she criticized my work harshly! Her view was that it was far too short, and should be at least twice as long, for the tree is one of the most powerful archetypes and should not be underestimated. This helped me enormously! To not be overwhelmed by the symbolism of the tree and thereby lose sight of the whole dream, we must forego such detail here, however.

176 C. G. Jung, *The Visions Seminars I,* Jung also sums up the relationship to the human psyche as follows: «Therefore the tree appears as a symbol wherever it is a matter of that spiritual development which is needed in order to reconcile pairs of opposites, or to settle a conflict», p. 513.

177 See C. G. Jung, *The Visions Seminars I,* p. 513.

Let's turn our attention now to the woman and the tree, which are linked in the dream. We recognize the fusion of these two archetypal images in the many nature goddesses or tree goddesses, such as the great goddess Isis/Hathor, who was also depicted as a tree on reliefs and tomb paintings in Ancient Egypt.[178]

Great mother goddesses were often depicted as trees. The Sumerian-Babylonian goddess Ishtar and numerous other Semitic goddesses of love and mother goddesses took the form of trees. In its maternal aspect, the tree also became a symbol of the original homeland, of paradise lost.[179]

For many peoples, special trees have a feminine or maternal quality.[180] Folklore reveals that particularly sacred, protected trees were embraced by pregnant women or visited during childbirth. It is said that Buddha's mother Maya gave birth to him at the foot of a tree. Apollo and Artemis are said to have been born after their mother Letho touched two trees. According to folklore, even children are born from trees. In certain places in Switzerland, for example, there was a so-called 'Kindlibaum' [a 'child-tree'] from which children were supposed to be born. Many trees, especially hollow ones, were seen to have a maternal quality and were therefore protected and revered.[181]

As a maternal symbol, the tree bestows secret wisdom. Obvious examples are the tree of knowledge in the Garden of Eden, or the mythological story of the world ash tree Iggdrasil upon which the Germanic god Odin hung for nine days to gain wisdom. In Christian legend, the cross becomes both the tree of life and the tree of death.[182] In some depictions, Christ hangs from a green, fruit-bearing tree. Here the tree is both the mother of life and death. In her epic work on symbolism in fairy tales, Marie-Louise von Franz says that within the psyche, the tree

178 R. Abt, "The Tree". In: R. Abt, I. Bosch, V. Mackrell, *Dream Child,* p. 123–158. See also: J. Brosse, *Mythologie der Bäume.*

179 Compare M.-L. von Franz, *Archetypal Symbols in Fairytales. The Profane and Magical World* (Vol. 1 of the Collected Works of M.-L. von Franz), p. 208 ff. (§ 521 ff).

180 C. G. Jung, *Alchemical Studies,* [CW 13], § 418 f.

181 See M. Eliade, *The Sacred and the Profane,* "The Sacredness of Nature and Cosmic Religion," p. 116 ff.

182 C. G. Jung, *Symbols of Transformation,* [CW 5], Fig. 71, § 349.

Fig. 30: C. G. Jung's tree in Bollingen.

stands for both a life-giving and a death-bringing principle. Furthermore, in its maternal aspect, it is a symbol for matter (lat. *mater* = mother), i.e., for the basic substance of the world – the basic substance of nature, the basis of life, indeed, the origin of all life.[183]

The encroachment of bushes or neglect of nature in the dream could therefore indicate our general neglect of the spiritual basis of life in our modern age. The dreamer tells us that in the area where the dreamer is staying nature was previously cultivated and cared for. Our farming ancestors, who could not have survived without observing the laws of nature, probably had a more 'cultivated,' considerate, and careful relationship with nature than we do today. While we cover fertile land with concrete to build our roads and houses, remote mountain areas are becoming depopulated, and land that was once cleared, used, and cared for in harmony with nature is now growing wild.

Understood symbolically as a dream image, this means that in earlier times, natural, spiritual content received a certain amount of attention and consideration within the framework of culture, religion, and tradition. This framework represented, if you like, a vessel for spiritual content. There was an awareness of spiritual forces, of the good and evil demons in human nature. Sagas, fairy tales, biblical stories, and legends, which used to be part of one's general cultural heritage, are all illustrations of spiritual realities that reflect our own inner nature. In our modern, technological age, we are inundated with and overwhelmed by outside impressions from morning to night, and our life as an individual is in danger of being completely lost within the masses. Our cultural asset of natural, spiritual content, which was able to reflect our own inner nature, is increasingly threatened with 'oblivion': it is forgotten, disregarded, and underestimated. Fortunately, the tree in the dream is healthy and has green leaves.

Now let us consider the snake. There is movement within the static situation. From where the tree and the woman stand, a snake suddenly shoots toward the dreamer. You could say that nature itself, the unconscious, reacts to the one who recognizes the situation. This makes sense because only as individuals is it possible for us to understand the

183 See M.-L. von Franz, *Archetypal Symbols in Fairytales. The Profane and Magical Worlds* (Vol. 1 of the Coll. Works of M.-L. von Franz), p. 211 (§ 528), with reference to KHM Nr. 123.

full extent of our alienation from the natural foundations of our existence. Only as an individual is it possible for one to recognize this contrast to one's own unconscious nature into which one has fallen and bring it up into the light of consciousness. This is why Jung placed the individual at the centre of all his efforts. It is within the individual, within one's own psyche, that the underestimation, the neglect, and the destruction of our own inner nature begins, which then contributes to the general problem in outer nature, in the outside world.

No government, no philosophy, no system of thought, no matter how sophisticated, can fulfil the task of becoming aware of one's own alienation from one's inner nature, with the resulting dangerous reactions on the part of the unconscious. Such dreams are a hint, a warning, an invitation to the conscious mind to grapple with the underlying problem and the dangers it brings to the collective, to the community, to society. This is why we pay attention to archetypal dreams. In the unconscious psyche, we find not only destructive but also healing tendencies toward renewal, as we saw in the ancient Egyptian myth of the underworld journey and its renewal of the sun god.

We know from the Bible that the snake symbolically belongs to the female-maternal tree. The story of the serpent in the tree in the Garden of Eden who seduces Eve relates Adam and Eve's inevitable expulsion from the paradisiacal state of unconsciousness: it is the beginning of the development of consciousness. No matter how much God appears to be annoyed by their deed and chooses to punish them both for it, their deed nevertheless seems to be God-ordained, to be in accordance with the course of nature. This story establishes a close connection between the serpent and the devil: in our Christian myth, it is the serpent who does the tempting. In alchemy, this aspect is represented by the *serpens mercurii*, the serpent of Mercury, the cunning and deceitful god Mercurius, as we mentioned earlier in the dream of the ox-child.[184] With such ambiguous characteristics, the outcome in the dream of this encounter with the snake is initially quite uncertain. But then the snake coils itself around the dreamer in an almost loving way. It behaves in a quite surprising manner. The characteristics attributed to snakes outlined below might explain why.

184 C. G. Jung, *Alchemical Studies* [CW 13], §416.

As I mentioned earlier, a snake's ability to shed its old skin and to reveal a new, shiny skin underneath made it a symbol of transformation, a symbol of eternal life, and of the constant renewal of nature. The serpent, then, has a role to play in creation. In the Greek-Orphic tradition, the original creator god Phanes (his older name is Eros) is depicted with a serpent entwined around him. Phanes is a bringer of light who emerged from the world egg of Chronos (time) and Ananke (fate). This connection with the creator god affords the serpent a cosmic dimension that is connected to the creation of the world, i.e., to the dawn of consciousness.

Another example can be found in the cult of Mithras, who was a kind of sun god. In the first three centuries in Rome, there was a lion-headed god, with a serpent entwined around his body, with its head resting upon his forehead (*deus leontocephalus)*. This god was called Aion, which means a long period of time, an age, an aeon, (gr. Aion = eternity). Everything is created in time, and time is identical with creation, for time changes everything and constantly creates anew.[185]

If I understand Jung correctly, in this figure of Aion, solar nature and unconsciousness, symbolized in the animal head of the god, is complemented by the feminine earthy spirit of the serpent, a symbol of new creation. As Jung points out, the time of the Mithras cult was a time of disorientation in which people had lost their direction and their values in a way that is reflective of today, and a completely new world began. Too much sun – too much rationality – combined with animalistic, i.e., unconscious, predatory instinctuality – represented by the lion's head – equates with an unnatural and one-sided attitude, both then as now. It leads to nature having to give way to humankind and its needs. Therefore, the snake is connected to this god.

As we have seen, the dream is more about the neglect of the land – about "the reassertion of nature," i.e., the overgrowth of land once cultivated, the encroachment of wild vegetation, which is nature taking back its own. In 'overgrown' i.e., abandoned land, there are usually snakes. The image of neglected nature which was at one time cultivated corresponds on a psychological level to a relapse from a more civilized state

185 See C. G. Jung, *The Visions Seminars II,* p. 1042 f.

Fig. 31: Depiction of Aion, mithraic, late Roman cult figure with key and/or staff as guardian to the afterworld, Musei Vaticani.

of consciousness into a state of unconsciousness from which unexpected, and possibly dangerous, snake impulses and emotions can emerge. The dream is concerned with this collective problem.

The snake approaches from the woman by the tree. Not only tree and woman, but also snake and woman have always seemed to belong together! We say of a woman that she is like a snake, but this rarely applies to a man! There were pre-Christian snake goddesses everywhere in the Near East. For example, Ishtar, the goddess with the attributes of a snake and a dove, can be found as early as the third millennium B.C.[186] In antiquity, the serpent became a symbol of the earth, which in turn was thought to be female.[187] In mythological contexts, the snake belongs to the earthy, dark side of the female goddess, or nature. One of the most terrifying, very ancient snake goddesses in Greece was Echidna, who is said to have been worshipped in Phrygian Hierapolis (a region in modern-day Turkey), a volcanic region where the otherwise hidden life of the earth came to light in the form of hot springs and vapours.[188]

It is through the archetypal symbols of snake, tree, and woman, that we try to get closer to a psychological understanding of the dream. In this man's dream, the woman represents the archetype of the anima, the "mistress soul," – in psychological terms, she is the embodiment of spiritual/mental life. The anima is connected to the tree which, as mentioned earlier, can be seen as the basic substance of the world – the basic substance of nature. If its symbolism merges with that of the tree, this suggests that spiritual life and the whole natural basis of life belong together. If one or the other is neglected, this can provoke, according to the dream, an unpredictable and dangerous reaction from the deep layers of the collective unconscious. This, then, is the snake.

But what is the connection between the anima and the snake? The anima itself is often depicted as a kind of half-animal creature. Psychologically, this means that it is precisely because of her animal nature that the anima functions as a mediator between the unconscious

186 See A. Schweizer: "Schlangenträume". In: E. Hornung, A. Schweizer, *Die Weisheit der Schlange,* p. 144.

187 C. G. Jung, *Symbols of Transformation,* [CW 5], § 155.

188 See A. Jaffé, *Bilder und Symbole aus E. T. A. Hoffmanns Märchen 'Der Goldene Topf',* p. 344.

and consciousness, in this dream between the snake and the dream ego. The dream seems to indicate that in this situation, one's behaviour toward the unconscious can be right or not. Either way, the unconscious is clearly interested in bringing about a change, for it decides to take the initiative: the snake approaches the dreamer of its own accord.

In this dream, too, it is important to remain calm within the snake's embrace to prevent the dark side of the unconscious – to prevent fear, panic, depression, poisoning, 'suffocating' emotion, all-consuming passion, illness, or any neurotic symptom that robs the individual of their mental and spiritual freedom – from taking over. Even if one does not know what it has in mind, the dreamer must be able to trust that the snake has nothing evil in mind. One only knows that it has something to do with this neglected, 'overgrown' nature, and that it is not hostile. No matter how uncanny it may appear in the moment, one needs to uphold an open, relaxed attitude towards the unconscious.

The archetypal symbolism of the dream shows how very deep the problem of our human relationship with nature goes. Indeed, it goes much deeper than our best efforts to protect nature today. The historical roots of the problem go back a long way. Our relationship to nature, to plants and animals, expressed everywhere in the cults of the great mother goddesses, disappeared completely in the patriarchal dogma of Christianity. As a result, the feminine values of feeling, of the soul, of female relatedness also largely disappeared from within the framework of recognized values. Today, particularly in the Western world, these same feminine values eke out an inauthentic existence as a kind of emotional moralism that distorts relationships, exacerbates the opposites of good and evil, and promotes an unrealistic world view.

Alchemy responded to the problem of the feminine and nature that remains unsolved in Christianity. Today, it is a matter of trusting and respecting nature, which wants to make itself felt in the human psyche, and of finding the right way to deal with it. The serpent that entwines itself around the dreamer is both the abysmal, cold-blooded, dark, and poisonous danger of the devouring side of outer and inner nature, and the potential for transformation, renewal, healing, and rebirth.

The snake is gnosis – knowledge – that emerges from nature, from our inner experience itself, says Jung. This is thinking that comes from

Fig. 32: Goddess with snake. Ugarit, around 2500 B.C.

the gut, from the viscera, from the blood, as it were. And this type of thinking is in direct contrast to academic, intellectual thinking. «That is also why this process is so often described as a revelation, as an eruption by which the individual is overwhelmed. It is always a process that rests within itself. That's the meaning of the snake when one experiences it from within.»[189] It can manifest itself in a particular situation in a completely irrational way, for example, as a sudden, unexpected insight that is capable of fundamentally changing one's entire conscious attitude.

External measures and activities to protect nature and animals are, of course, extremely important and urgent. Many people are profoundly dedicated to this. But if one has a dream like this, it seems to indicate that there should or could be a change within the person at the same time. Then it would be a matter of taking care of the inner 'neglect.'

Being lovingly embraced by such a powerful snake is undoubtedly a formative experience that cannot be described as anything other than fateful. We sense that here, too, the appearance of the snake signifies a powerful impulse from the unconscious, a 'warning shot' to one's conscious mind and, at the same time, an invitation. Because the snake is bound up with the creative, it can bring forth unexpected solutions and thoughts. It is a creative instinct that can initiate a new spiritual direction that both arises and is sustained from within. Medicine men all over the world festoon themselves with snake symbols![190]

But if a creative urge, as embodied by the snake, is not taken seriously, it can become dangerous. We discussed this earlier in connection with the octopus. Creative people are usually in danger of being threatened by the poisonous snake of depression and fragmentation, or of being spiritually suffocated, as it were, if they are unwilling or unable to fulfil their creative task. Jung was not exaggerating when he spoke of the creative demon that had haunted him throughout his life.[191] In archaic societies, such dreams were perceived as shamanistic dreams of initiation, for example, which revealed the dreamer's inevitable destiny as a healer or spiritual leader of his tribe. These dreams were important to the whole tribe: they were

189 C. G. Jung, *Children's Dreams,* p. 261 f.

190 B. Hannah, *The Archetypal Symbolism of Animals,* p. 226.

191 C. G. Jung, *Memories, Dreams, Reflections*, p. 358 f.

shared publicly in a palaver. We do not know what consequences that this encounter with the snake in his dreams had for the dreamer.

We may assume that the dreamer knew beforehand that nature needed to be protected. Nevertheless, it makes a difference if you get the message by having a poisonous snake coiled around your body rather than reading about it in a newspaper or book, or if you are asked to take action by politicians through rules and bans. Such an inner experience can completely change and realign a person's attitude. On the other hand, if one has a dream like this, there is the great danger of seeing oneself as saviour of the world in an extraverted way. This is why the dream closes with the dreamer going back down the mountain, hiding his experience from the people, and doing gymnastics with them in his underpants. This would appear to be a foolproof remedy against inflation, overconfidence, and prophecy!

After I had finished writing this section, I came across an ancient Egyptian text that had been recorded in hieroglyphic script around 4000 years ago.[192] To put it in a nutshell, the story tells of a shipwrecked man who was stranded on a paradisical island. After making an offering to thank the gods, a mighty, gold-covered serpent with eyebrows of lapis lazuli appeared. It was the mistress of the island who, enraged, initially threatened to destroy him. Throwing himself to the ground in front of her, he told her the story of the shipwreck in which all his comrades had perished. She then reassured him that a god had brought him to this rich island and that he would be able to live there in peace until a ship arrived to bring him back to his homeland, safe and sound. And that is how it happened. Then, as the serpent had predicted, this paradise island sank beneath the waves forever.

This tale of the shipwrecked man is probably the oldest written story of a miraculous rescue snake. It later appears in countless parallel stories in religions and folklore, for example, in antiquity in *The Odyssey*, or in the story of *Sinbad the Sailor* in the *Tales of 1001 Nights*. To not be destroyed by the divine life serpent, and to bring out its helpful side,

192 G. Lanzckowski, *Die Geschichte des Schiffbrüchigen,* p. 360–371. And: M. Lapidus, *La quête de l'île merveilleuse.*

the serpent must be respected and revered. The fact that this motif of the helpful snake has spread over four millennia and found its way into the traditions of so many peoples[193] and into the dreams of people today, gives us a sense of the timelessness of the archetypal basic structures of the unconscious psyche. Then as now, these archetypes determined and continue to have a determining effect upon our lives.

I wanted to close this long chapter on snake dreams at this point, but it did not seem to want to let me go. Out of the blue, I received the following dream. It features a cow and a snake, the two themes I had selected, perhaps quite inappropriately, without really knowing why. It was dreamt by a 6o year old woman with Jewish roots who had had a very difficult life. She had this dream when she was about 21 years old, and it accompanied her throughout her life. Even if I cannot do it justice with a detailed interpretation, I would like to bring this work to a close by citing it. The dreams of the cow and snake we discussed earlier may give us some idea of its depth and meaning.

Dream 18: The black cobra snake

I saw a young woman in the middle of a wheat field. She was tired of men and had decided to have sexual intercourse with a cow. I then see a big white cow and the young woman together having sex in this huge golden wheat field.

The scene changes, and I saw a pregnant woman laying on a bed. She seemed to be in labour but remained still and quiet. I saw her huge, rounded belly. There was not much light in this small room, but I could feel somehow that it was in India. Some people were around the bed, waiting, in silence. I was among them. There was a kind of expectation.

Suddenly, I saw the baby coming out from between her open legs. But at closer inspection, I saw that what was coming out of her body was a huge black cobra snake, almost my size. Everybody left the room swiftly. I saw the snake standing in front of me and I also ran out of the room in fear.

I ran inside a patio in which stood a leafless tree, with many branches. When I saw that the snake was chasing me, I decided to climb up the tree.

193 See further references on the subject in M. Lapidus, *La quête de l'île merveilleuse.*

I was up there, hanging on the branches, when I heard a masculine voice asking me to come down. It was the cobra, standing beside the tree, but I was too scared to go down. At that point, I suddenly realized that all the branches were full of small black poisonous snakes. I had no other choice but to climb down the tree and face the big cobra. She then told me that I had to die because I had witnessed the birth of a sacred being. She was going to kill me. I started to beg her to spare my life. The cobra agreed to let me live on one condition: that I had to search and find some kind of Jewish rituals for her. When I agreed, the snake told me to place my arm inside her mouth, which I did. She bit me with some kind of non-poisonous back teeth. Thus, the pact was sealed.

First let's discuss the huge, golden wheat field. In primordial times, humans had largely subsisted on plants and roots, and by hunting. The cultivation of grain was a tremendous cultural achievement. Grain symbolized the miraculous, repeated growth of vital food from the earth, where it appeared to be lost and buried. Vegetation gods such as Osiris, Tammuz, Attis etc., embodied this mystery of death and resurrection.[194] In ancient Egypt, this idea took a special form: Osiris himself was described as grain – as wheat or barley – which is why grain was sprouted on the body of the dead. He embodied life that survives death, i.e., something psychic "which is beyond the opposites of life and death," as Marie-Louise von Franz puts it.[195] It is therefore likely that the ripe wheat field has to do with a process of transformation in a broader sense, in the collective unconscious.

The white cow, which paradoxically helps to bring forth a new birth, is reminiscent of the nurturing Hathor cow, as well as the white cow in the first of our cow dreams. She is the feminine, instinctive principle of the unconscious, with which the woman wants to connect, for the male Logos principle is evidently increasingly exhausted. "She was tired of men," the dream says. If the relationship between the masculine and feminine principles in the psyche is disturbed, the unconscious, instinctive functioning of the psyche is disturbed. As a result, the nurturing 'lower' goddess, embodied by the cow, begets a monster (the alchemical *serpens*).

194 M.-L. von Franz, *On Dreams and Death,* p. 37.
195 Ibid., p. 13.

This is the collective situation of our time in which the dominance of the masculine-rational principle of consciousness has, more than ever before, led the world to the edge of the abyss. We do not know whether, even with all our intellectual efforts, we can prevent our own destruction. The ideas of our leaders often seem too far-fetched and unrealistic, the quicksand of the zeitgeist too easy, and certain goals of science too frighteningly inhuman.[196] Even in his time Jung warned, «Reason without tradition and without any basis in instinct is not protected from absurdity.»[197] This deficit activates a dangerous tendency in the unconscious that we have yet to recognize. Jung goes on to say: «One does not realize yet that when an archetype is unconsciously constellated and not consciously understood, one is *possessed by it* and forced to its fatal goal.» We cannot help but associate the black cobra with this. Instead of a new leader, a new messiah, or a new saviour that people seem to be waiting for in dreams and in reality, the unconscious produces a deadly threat, a diabolical monster. The archetypal power of this dream must have deeply frightened the young woman.

The dreamer associated India with an Indian goddess who gives birth to a snake. Why India? We have no knowledge about the dreamer's personal relationship to the Indian culture and religion. In India, all cows are sacred: they roam the streets freely and may not be slaughtered. Hinduism has hundreds of gods and goddesses who all convey a rich and colourful picture of the many and varied characteristics of the human psyche. Perhaps India here represents the hope of being able to integrate the encroaching evil into the existing, relatively open religious system that is India. If so, this does not appear to be a success, for what is born is too terrible. People run away in panic, and the dreamer is pursued by the black cobra.

She desperately tries to climb a tree, but it offers her no protection. On the contrary, it is poisoned by the small black snakes on its branches, just as the whole situation seems poisoned and inescapable. The tree, a feminine symbol and an image of the inner growth process which follows its own laws from birth to death, has turned against the conscious ego. But

196 See the efforts being made in scientific fields on transhumanism and posthumanism.

197 C.G. Jung, *Letters, Vol. II:* Letter of 14. 9. 1960 to Miguel Serrano, p. 594.

for us, this dream is primarily a dream of collective significance. Thus, we could say that because consciousness has a wrong attitude, the 'maternal' unconscious [the mater], the archetypal basis of matter, has turned into the toxic, exuberant materialism that characterizes our time. This is where we stand today. Contrary to the optimism of the last two centuries, technological progress now represents more of a threat than a way out. It is doubtful that further technological development will save us. The situation seems hopeless. Will the unconscious destroy us? In fear and trepidation, many people are now asking themselves if there even is a way out.

In this seemingly hopeless situation, the black cobra's intention becomes clear. Its 'masculine' voice summons the dream ego to confront it. According to the dream, the reason for the deadly threat from the unconscious lies in the fact that it is apparently forbidden, – on pain of death, as the dream says –, to witness the divine birth, the emergence of the great evil.

We recognize this motif from many fairy tales, in which, for example, it is forbidden to open a certain door. Such a prohibition is regularly violated in fairy tales and is often severely punished. It is dangerous to reveal the innermost secret of a deity. The psychological meaning behind this prohibition is, as Marie-Louise von Franz explains in her interpretation of the fairy tale *In the Black Woman's Castle,* that the «human ego is set apart from the divine-demonic figure in such a way as to ward off an inflation or an explosion.»[198] It is about the «safeguarding of the human boundary with the numinous,» a need to protect oneself from one's own emotion (panic) and the emotion of the deity.[199] A person can be overwhelmed and burst apart if they are assimilated by an archetype.[200] In the case of the black snake, this would be a dangerous unconsciousness, the danger of being overwhelmed by the unconscious shadow characteristics of depression, aggression, panic, and other unconscious complexes. The dreamer falls into this terrible threat in the dream through no fault of her own. On a collective level, an 'open door' like this means that entire groups or nations are 'open' to suggestion and mass psychosis.[201]

198 M.-L. von Franz, *Archetypal Dimensions of the Psyche*, p. 187.

199 Ibid., p. 200.

200 Ibid., p. 195.

201 C. G. Jung, *Aion,* [CW 9/II], § 391, Footnote 79.

We have seen that the snake is both a symbol of renewal and the embodiment of evil, as it seems to be here. Like Job in the Old Testament, the dreamer is "confronted with the inner divine opposites (Yahweh / Satan)."[202] In the same way Job is distressed by his terrifying experience of God, the dreamer is terrified by her experience of the 'divine birth' of the black snake. The experience of great evil could kill her. In concrete terms, this means that she could become psychotic. The young woman must have been in great psychological danger at the time of the dream.

There is only one way out for her: she must fulfil the condition of the dark deity, the black cobra within her psyche. From then on, the question as to what this might mean was at the centre of her life. But when a 21-year-old woman has such a big dream, we must assume that it goes beyond her individual personality and addresses a collective problem that she alone cannot solve. We cannot know why she and not someone else had this dream. It is probably part of her particularly difficult fate in some way. Jung says that such experiences of God can or should affect people both inwardly and outwardly, without rational re-interpretation and mitigation.[203]

The male, black cobra will only spare the dreamer if she seeks and finds a Jewish ritual for it. Not knowing the dreamer, her associations, or her family history, this strange request remains a puzzle to us. We only know that she comes from a Jewish family on her father's side. How is this connection between the snake and the Jewish religion of the past to be understood? In his Visions Seminars, Jung discusses the dream of a woman with a black snake. There, he says that the black serpent «would be the woman's connection with the earth, and that would be at the same time her connection with the past. The ancestors are living in the earth; they are buried there. The life of the earth is our past, and psychologically the snake means our connection with the past existence, with the primeval forests and caves.»[204] We can see that her ego consciousness has been set a task that leads into her past and, at the same time, into her unconscious. At this moment, this seems to be the only thing that can appease the great evil looming.

202 M.-L. von Franz, "In the Black Woman's Castle." In: *Archetypal Dimensions of the Psyche.* p. 198.

203 C. G. Jung, *Answer to Job.* [CW 11], § 562.

204 C. G. Jung, *The Visions Seminars I,*. p. 276.

In contrast to the Christian image of God in the New Testament as a 'loving God,' the Jewish God Yahweh is a light/dark God who, in his dark aspect, is a fiery, unjust, irascible God who demands unconditional obedience from his people. Does perhaps the archaic, animalistic, serpent god at this moment require a further development toward the Jewish image of God, which is closer to him than the Christian image is? How does Judaism deal with this dark aspect of God? As Jung writes in a letter, the people of the Old Testament were able to address themselves to an unreliable God.[205] Do the Jewish rituals that the serpent demands have anything to do with this? Or do they have more to do with the Jewish Job who, according to the Bible, when Satan destroyed his life and his family on behalf of Yahweh, put his hand over his mouth in wise humility?[206] Is the dream setting a fateful task for the dreamer, asking her to recognize the dark side of God, to endure it through her devotion to God, to grapple with it respectfully and, in this way, ultimately to contribute to God's possible transformation or awareness? The golden wheat field and the white cow seem to point to such a profound possibility of transformation. If this were so, this dream would give the dreamer's sorrowful life a meaning that goes far beyond her personal life.[207]

Jung has shown that religious customs, rituals, and taboos psychologically correspond to the restrictive forms of instincts. In nature, excessive instincts are hostile to life. We can readily observe how animals behave instinctively in accordance with the rules that govern their species. As human consciousness develops, such restrictive forms of instinct no longer seem to apply. «Thus, it appears that religion was originally a psychological regulatory system, which ordered our instincts and drives. Only when a religious system hardens into a rigid formalism does it become

205 C.G. Jung, *Letters, Vol. II,* Letter to Elined Kotschnig, 30.6.1956, p.315. And: A. Jaffé, *Streiflichter zu Leben und Denken C.G. Jungs,* p.112: «Von den Juden kann man lernen, wie man zu einem ambivalenten Gott betet.» («From the Jewish people one can learn how to address an ambivalent God in prayer.»)

206 See C.G. Jung, *Answer to Job,* [CW 11].

207 C.G. Jung, *Letters, Vol. II*, Letter of June 26, 1956, p.310 f. «Yahweh's amorality or notorious injustice changes only with the Incarnation into the exclusive goodness of God. This transformation is connected with his becoming man and therefore exists only if it is made real *through the conscious fulfilment of God's will in man.*»

antagonistic to the instincts and negative.»[208] With churches remaining empty and believers becoming scarce, there is much evidence today that reveals how rigid and alienated from life our Christian religious system has become. The dream would seem to have us understand that religious renewal first requires an understanding of, and a way of dealing with, the dark side of God, an approach that has been ritually developed in Judaism.

As we have seen, the snake is a symbol of God, a symbol of the self, that encompasses all possible opposites. Why, though, does it adopt such a frightening form here? Marie-Louise von Franz writes, «From the fact that the (S)self appears in animal form in the dreams and visions of medicine men and creative individuals, it is clear that it is first perceived as a purely instinctive unconscious force, greater and more powerful than the ego but entirely unconscious. It embodies the complete wisdom of nature yet does not possess the light of human consciousness.»[209] The self, then, often emerges first as an ambivalent, or even dangerous, instinctual activity.

To bear witness to the birth of the dark deity is dangerous, the dream says. From a psychological point of view, this equates to becoming aware of the dangerous and dark side of the unconscious. Apparently, this is a sacrilege, a transgression of human boundaries, which according to mythological stories is always punished by the gods. Nevertheless, this psychological process seems to be intentional on the part of the unconscious. In the dream, it happens without the dreamer's intervention and without any blame on her part. It seems that the dark deity wants to be recognized and assimilated by the human ego, i.e. it wants to become conscious. But such a realization also poses a deadly threat. The darkness can poison or crush one, engulfing one in cynicism or depression. The dream, however, shows a way out of this seemingly hopeless situation.

To place one's arm in the mouth of the black cobra and to be bitten by it in a 'non-poisonous' way is to seal a binding pact with the devil, so to speak, with the dangerous side of the self. The bite of the black cobra lays its mark upon one's ego-consciousness, obliging it to perform a task. To not sink into the masses and despair over her difficult fate, the dreamer

208 M.-L. von Franz, "Individuation and Social Relation in Jungian Psychology." In: *Archetypal Dimensions of the Psyche*, p. 252.

209 Ibid., 252.

Fig. 33: Brahmanaspati, 1916. The snake as symbol of the self in C.G. Jung's *Red Book: Liber Novus*, p. 54.

needs a religious, 'God-devoted' relationship with the unconscious. «Evil has become a determinant reality. [...] We must learn to handle it, since it is here to stay [...]», Jung states.[210] In this way, the dark deity that emerges through the serpent's birth is appeased and refrains from destroying the distraught ego.

But what is the reason for the black cobra's enigmatic demand to seek and find some kind of Jewish ritual for her? I couldn't make any sense of it.

Then I came across the following paragraph in Jung's letters, which suddenly seemed to shed light on the last section of the dream. Jung refers to a treatise of the Lurianic Kabbalah, namely the breaking of the vessels and the people's help in restoring them. «Here the thought emerges for the first time that man must help God to repair the damage wrought by the Creation. For the first time man's cosmic responsibility is acknowledged.»[211] The dream of the black cobra, which demands that the dreamer find Jewish rituals for it, seems to depict the plight of the deity and the importance of human consciousness in reuniting the opposites that have been torn apart. In this myth, the vessels that broke when God wanted to create the world point to the tearing apart of the opposites of reason and instinct, of light and darkness, which happens with every expansion of consciousness.

In a ritual, a person is addressing the divine or, in psychological terms, an overpowering spiritual content to which they thereby afford their attention and a place within their own life. For the dreamer, referring to the dark serpent spirit in the ritual could mean incorporating it into her image of God, as it were, in accordance with her Jewish roots. We can barely imagine how difficult this would be given that the dark god had made life as difficult as he had for her.

210 C.G. Jung, *Memories, Dreams, Reflections,* p.329.

211 C.G. Jung, *Letters*, Vol. II, Letter to James Kirsch, 16.2.1954, p.154 f. See also Letter to Rev. Erastus Evans, 17.2.1954, p.155 ff. And Letter to Dr. James Kirsch, 18.11.1952, p.91 ff., footnote 4: «The *kelipoth,* 'shards' or 'shells,' are the daemonic forces of evil. According to the Kabbalist Isaac Luria (1534–72), they originated in the "breaking of the vessels" of the *sefiroth* which could not contain the power of God. The world of the *kelipoth* is the counterpole to the world of the *sefiroth*.»

Like the dreamer in the above dream of the rescue snake, here too it is a single person who seems to be destined to carry out his or her own task, which the process of becoming conscious sets him or her. In such so-called great dreams, however, the relationship of the individual to the collective, to human society, is also expressed in the broadest sense beyond the personal. Ultimately, it is about defusing the now terribly exacerbated collective conflict between the consciousness lost in the rational world and the feminine-creative, instinctive unconscious in all its dangerous ambiguity. This conflictual opposition reflects the world's armed conflicts, which threaten us today more than ever.

Jung believed that at the deepest level of the archetypes, people the world over behave in the same way and are connected.[212] Therefore, wherever an archetype is activated in the sense of becoming conscious, its effect can manifest anywhere and in anyone. As Jung writes, «If the archetype, which is universal, i.e., identical with itself always and anywhere, is properly dealt with in one place only, it is influenced as a whole, i.e., simultaneously and everywhere.»[213] Ultimately, this signifies a tremendous revaluation of the individual and of one's individual responsibility, and perhaps, too, it provides us with a reason to hope?

I am aware that there was no room to manoeuvre amidst the powerful images of this and the preceding dreams we have discussed. Much remains uncertain and we can readily admit that we can usually only grasp a glimmer of the meaning of a dream. This is especially true when ancient symbolism appears in modern dream material, which we have somehow to grasp and integrate. Because snake dreams occur frequently and always give rise to concern and questions, perhaps it has been helpful and worthwhile to take a closer look at them, even if, as it seems to me, they are particularly difficult to understand because of the snake's own uncanny and strange nature. They are invariably about essential things, and sometimes, as we have seen, they are even about fate.

212 This is based on the idea of synchronicity, as understood by the ancient Chinese. Confucius said that if someone sat alone in a room and had the right thoughts, the right thoughts would be heard a thousand miles away. «Everything is contained in the oneness, such that everything is connected with everything else in a meaningful way.» In: "Forever Jung" (Conversations with Marie-Louise von Franz by James Cott) in: J. Cott, *Visions and Voices, New York* 1995.

213 C.G. Jung, *Letters, Vol. II,* 14.09.1960, to Miguel Serrano, p.595.

In any event, whenever we encounter a snake, we would do well to never underestimate it and to show it our cautious respect. The snake is always a particularly powerful expression of what is within our psyche, and thus of our "forgotten language of instincts." The symbol of the snake can complement and compensate our conscious, rational approach that so easily succumbs to outside impressions and suggestions, and it has the power to reestablish our psychic/spiritual equilibrium.[214]

214 C.G. Jung, *The Symbolic Life* [CW 18], § 474.

Appendix

1. Bibliography

Abt, Sabine: *Der Flammenhimmel. Die Geschichte einer wunderbaren Reise*, Einsiedeln 2021.

Abt, Theodor: *Introduction to Picture Interpretation. According to C. G. Jung,* Zürich 2005.

Abt Theodor; Hornung, Erik: *Knowledge for the Afterlife. The Egyptian Amduat – A Quest for Immortality,* Zürich 2003.

Abt-Baechi, Regina: *Animals and Animal Dreams. The Cat, The Dog, the Horse,* Zurich 2011.

– *Animals and Animal Dreams II. The Fish,* Zurich 2019.

– *Princess and Magic Horse. Psychological Interpretation of three Fairy Tales,* Zurich 2013.

– *The Saint and the Pig*, Zürich 2015.

Abt-Baechi, Regina; Bosch, Irmgard; Mackrell, Vivian: *Dream Child,* Einsiedeln 2000.

Bible, see Holy Bible, King James Version.

Birkhäuser-Oeri, Sibylle: *Mother Figures in Fairy Tales. A Jungian Examination of the Mother Archetype and the Mother Complex as they Appear in Well-Known Fairy Tales.* Unabridged version, edited by M.-L. von Franz, Einsiedeln 2023.

Bleek, W.H.I.; Lloyd, L. C.: *Specimens of Bushmen Folklore,* Einsiedeln 2001.

Brosse, Jaques: *Mythologie der Bäume,* Olten and Freiburg i. B. 1990.

Caillois, Roger: *Der Krake. Versuch über die Logik des Imaginativen,* New York 1969.

Chevallier, Jean; Gheerbrant, Alain: *Dictionnaire des Symboles,* Paris 1969.

Cott, Jonathan: "Forever Jung" (Conversations with Marie-Louise von Franz by James Cott, Interview). In: .J Cott: *Visions and Voices,* New York 1995.

Edinger, Edward F.: *The Creation of Consciousness. Jung`s Myth for Modern Man*, Toronto 1984.

Eliade Mircea: *A History of Religious Ideas*, 1976.

– *Archaic Techniques of Ecstasy,* Princeton 1974

– *The Sacred and the Profane,* New York 1959.

Ellis, Richard: *Seeungeheuer, Mythen, Fabeln und Fakten,* Basel 1997.

Englert-Faye, Curt: *Alpensagen*, Zürich 1941.

Foster, Craig; Reed, James: *My Octopus Teacher*. A film directed and written by Pippa Ehrlich and James Reed, produced by Craig Foster, starring Craig Foster and Tom Foster, Netflix Film 2020.

Godfrey-Smith, Peter: *Other minds. The Octopus and the Evolution of Intelligent Life*, London 2018.

Goethe, Johann Wolfgang von: *Faust Parts I + II,* translated by A. S. Kline Independent Publishing Platform, 2015.

Grimm, Gebrüder: *Kinder- u. Hausmärchen (KHM),* Düsseldorf, Köln 1958.

Gubernatis, Angelo de: *Die Tiere in der indogermanischen Mythologie,* Leipzig 1874, Reprint 1978.

Hannah, Barbara: *The Archetypal Symbolism of Animals,* Wilmette Ill. 2006.

– *C. G. Jung. His Life and Work. A biographical Memoir,* New York 1976.

Hannah, Barbara; von Franz, Marie-Louise: *Lectures on Jung's Aion, Wilmette, Ill. 2004 and Ashville 2015.*

Hartmann, H.; Müller, U.; Wyss, Ch.: *Sagen aus dem Berner Oberland,* Interlaken 1910 und 1985.

Hasler, Eveline: *Der Riese im Baum,* München 2004.

Hauser, Albert: *Das Neue kommt. Schweizer Alltag im 19. Jahrhundert,* Zürich 1989.

Hoffman-Krayer, E.; Bächtold-Stäubli, H.: *Handwörterbuch des deutschen Aberglaubens,* Bd. III. Berlin 1933, reprint 1987.

Holy Bible, King James Version, Oxford 1769.

Hornung, Erik: "Söhne der Erde. Schlangen im Diesseits und Jenseits der Ägypter". In: E. Hornung; A. Schweizer (Eds.): *Die Weisheit der Schlange.* Beiträge der Eranos Tagungen 2003 und 2004, Basel 2005.

I Ching, the book of Changes. Ed. by Richard Wilhelm, Princeton 2011.

Isler, Gotthilf: *Lumen Naturae,* Küsnacht 2000.

Jaffé, Aniela: *Bilder und Symbole aus E.T.A. Hoffmanns Märchen 'Der goldene Topf'.* In: C.G. Jung: *Gestaltungen des Unbewussten,* Zürich 1950.

– *C. G. Jung: Memories, Dreams, Reflections*, New York 1989.

– *Streiflichter zu Leben und Denken C. G. Jungs,* Aniela Jaffé nach Gesprächen mit C.G. Jung, Historischer Kommentar von Elena Fischli, Einsiedeln 2021.

Jung, Carl Gustav: *Aion, Researches into the Phenomenology of the Self,* [Collected Works 9.II], Princeton 1968.

– *Alchemical Studies,* [Collected Works 13], Princeton 1968.

– "Answer to Job", *in: Psychology and Religion, West and East,* [Collected Works 11], Princeton 1969.

– *Children's Dreams*, Philemon Series, Princeton 2008.

– *Civilization in Transition,* [Collected Works 10], Princeton 1970.

– *Deutsches Seminar 5.-10. Okt. 1931*, Unpublished manuscript, Stuttgart 1932.

– *Dream Analysis. Notes of the Seminar given 1928–30,* London 1984.

– *Dream Symbols of the Individuation Process,* ed. Suzanne Gieser, Princeton and Oxford 2019.

– *Letters* (2 Volumes: 1906–1961), ed. by Gerhard Adler in collaboration with Aniela Jaffé, London 1973, 1976.

– *Memories, Dreams, Reflections*. Recorded and edited by Aniela Jaffé, New York 1989.

– *Mysterium coniunctionis I* and *II* [Collected Works 14.1 and 14.2], Princeton 1963, 1970.

– *Psychology and Alchemy,* [Collected Works 12], Princeton 1968.

– *Psychology and Religion, West and East,* [Collected Works 11], Princeton 1969.

– *Symbols of Transformation,* [Collected Works 5], Princeton 1967.

– *The Archetypes and the Collective Unconscious,* [Collected Works 9 I], Princeton 1968.

– *The Symbolic Life; Miscellaneous Writings* [CW 18], Princeton 1976.

– *The Visions Seminars (2 Vols.)*, Princeton 1997.

Jung, Carl Gustav et al.: *Man and his Symbols*, London 1968.

Jung-Rauschenbach, Emma: *Animus and Anima,* New York 1957.

Keel, Othmar: *Das Recht der Bilder gesehen zu werden. Drei Fallstudien zur Methode der Interpretation altorientalischer Bilder*, Freiburg (Schweiz), Göttingen 1992.

Kerényi, Karl: *Der göttliche Arzt. Studien über Asklepios und seine Kultstätten,* Basel 1948.

Lanzckowski, G.: "Die Geschichte des Schiffbrüchigen. Versuch einer religionsgeschichtlichen Interpretation", *Zeitschrift der Deutschen Morgenländischen Gesellschaft,* No. 103, 1953.

Lapidus, Michel: *La Quête de l'île merveilleuse.* In the Egyptian Seminar of the University of Basel, Paris 1995.

Montgomery, Sy: *The Soul of an Octopus. A surprising Exploration into the Wonder of Consciousness,* London 2015.

Narby, Jeremy: *The cosmic Serpent. DNA and the Origins of Knowledge*, London 1999.

Reed, Alexander Wycliff: *Myths and Legends of Fiji*, Wellington, Auckland, Sidney 1967.

Reed, James; Foster, Craig: *My Octopus Teacher.* A film directed and written by Pippa Ehrlich and James Reed, produced by Craig Foster, starring Craig Foster and Tom Foster, Netflix Film 2020.

Renner, Eduard: *Goldener Ring über Uri,* Altdorf 1941, 2016.

Roscher, W. H.: *Lexikon der germanischen und römischen Mythologie,* Vol. 1 and 2, Hildesheim, New York 1978.

Schweizer, Andreas: "Schlangenträume". In: Erik Hornung, Andreas Schweizer (eds.): *Die Weisheit der Schlange. Beiträge der Eranos Tagungen 2003 und 2004*, Basel 2005.

Sooder, Melchior: *Zelleni us em Haslital.* Aus mündlicher Überlieferung aufgezeichnet, Basel 1943, Meiringen 1984.

Storl, Wolf-Dieter: *Einsichten und Weitblicke,* München 2020.

– *Unsere 5 heiligen Bäume,* München 2020.

– *Wir sind Geschöpfe des Waldes,* München 2019.

Von Franz, Marie-Louise:

– *Archetypal Dimensions of the Psyche,* Boston, London 1999.

– *Archetypal Patterns in Fairytales*, Toronto 1997.

– *Archetypal Symbols in Fairytales: The Profane and Magical Worlds* (Vol. 1) and *Arch. Symbols in Fairytales: The Maiden's Quest,* (Vol. 3 of the Collected Works of M.-L. von Franz), Asheville, 2021–2022.

– *C. G. Jung. His Myth in our Time,* Toronto 1998.

– *Creation Myths,* Boston, London 1995.

– *Commentary to M. Ibn Umail's Kitāb Ḥall ar-Rumūz, Book of the Explanation of the Symbols,* (Corpus Alchemicum Arabicum IA, CALA I A), ed. by Theodor Abt, Zürich 2006.

– *Conversations on Aion, in: B. Hannah, M.-L. von Franz, Lectures on Jung's Aion*, Wilmette, Ill. 2004.

– "Forever Jung" (Conversations with Marie-Louise von Franz by James Cott, Interview), see Jonathan Cott.

– *Individuation in Fairytales,* Boston, London 1971, Küsnacht 2013.

– *On Dreams and Death,* Chicago 1998.

– *Shadow and Evil in Fairytales*, Zürich, Küsnacht 2013.

– *The Feminine in Fairy Tales*, Boston, London 1993.

– *The Interpretation of Fairy Tales*, Boston, London 1996.

– *The Problems of the Puer Aeternus,* Toronto 2000.

– "The Process of Individuation". In: C.G. Jung et al.*: Man and his Symbols,* (see there), p. 158–229, with ch.: "The Anima, the woman within", p. 177–188; "The Animus, the man within", p. 189–192.

– *The Psychological Meaning of Redemption Motifs in Fairy Tales,* Toronto 1980, Küsnacht 2013.

Von Franz, Marie-Louise; Hannah, Barbara: *Lectures on Jung's Aion,* Asheville 2004, 2015.

Wagner, Barbara: "Der Oktopus", Symbolarbeit am C.G. Jung Institut, Küsnacht 2000 (not published).

Wesselsky, Albert: *Deutsche Märchen vor Grimm*, München, Wien 1942.

Wilhelm, Richard (Ed.): *The I Ching. The book of Changes*, Princeton 2011.

Zerling, Clemens; Bauer, Wolfgang: *Lexikon der Tiersymbolik,* München 2003.

2. List of Figures

The Cow

Fig. 1: Cow of the breed Brown Swiss. Photo by the author.

Fig. 2: Cows returning from a Swiss alp after the summer. Photo by the author.

Fig. 3: Head of the cult statue of the goddess Hathor. Burial temple of Hatschepsut, 1465 B.C., London, British Museum. In: *Die Welt der Pharaonen*. Ed. by Regine Schulz, Matthias Seidel, published by Könemann, p. 186.

Fig. 4: Cow goddess Hathor. Saqqara, 600–500 B.C., Kairo. In: *La Femme dans l'Egypte des Pharaons*, Genève 1986, Fig. 85.

Fig. 5: Worship of the cow goddess, Sarcophagus of Khonsu. 1295–1186. In: Erik Hornung, Betsy M. Bryn, *Quest for Immortality.* National Gallery of Art, Washington 2002, Fig. 68.

Fig. 6: Hathor cow in tomb of Seti I. Aquarelle made by R. Hay after 1824. In: E. Hornung: *Tal der Könige. Die Ruhestätte der Pharaonen,* Zurich and Munich, 1985, 4. Auflage 1988, p. 176, fig. 149, from British Library, Add. Mss. 29 820, f. 97.

Fig. 7: Golden pendant. Isis/Hathor, 1069–945 B.C., Egyptian Museum Kairo. In: Erik Hornung, Betsy M. Bryn, *Quest for Immortality.* National Gallery of Art, Washington 2002. Fig. 42.

Fig. 8: Germanic-nordic God. Bronze statuette, Reykjavik, National Museum, Hamlyn archives. In: Ives Bonnefoy, *Mythologies I,* Chicago, London 1991, p. 291.

Fig. 9: "Mercurius tricephalus" as Anthropos, 1676. In: C.G: Jung, *Psychology and Alchemie*, [Collected Works 12], § 70.

The Octopus

Fig. 10: Octopus. Foto Getty Images.

Fig. 11: Octopus, Netflix film: still.

Fig. 12: Octopus attacks a ship, according to Denys de Montfort. In: R. Ellis, *Seeungeheuer,* p. 254.

Fig. 13: Bluecurled kraken, postcard.

Fig. 14: Dakuwaqwa, the shark god battling against the Octopus. In: Island Time, *The Octopus – A Fijian Legend.*

The Snake

Fig. 15: Zeus Mailichios, relief, marble, about 400–375 BC., *Encyclopedia of Archetypal Symbolism.* Ed. by Beverly Moon, Boston, London 1991, p. 78.

Fig. 16: Watersnake, postcard.

Fig. 17: Pesttaler, Erzgebirge (1528), Dorotheum Wien.

Fig. 18: Snake at the cross, Abraham Eleazar: *Uraltes chymisches Werk,* Leipzig 1760, p. 329. In: Alexander Roob. *Alchemie und Mystik. Das hermetische Museum,* Köln 2006.

Fig. 19: Winged Uraeus snake, 20.th Dynasty. Valley of the Queens, Tomb of prince Amun-her Chepeschef, a son of Ramses III. Photo Jaques Livet. In: Philippe Germond, *Das Tier im Alten Ägypten,* München 2001, p. 177.

Fig. 20: Imperial tomb in the cathedral of Würzburg, Germany. Wood carving by Tillman Riemenschneider, 16.th century. In: Peter Dinzelbacher, *Himmel, Hölle, Heilige,* Darmstadt 2002, p. 65.

Fig. 21: Mereseger, goddess of death from Theben. Antikenmuseum Basel.

Fig. 22: Roman Statue of Asclepius, 150 A. C., Uffizi, Florence. Probably according to the cult statue created by Alkamenes at about 400 B.C. for the Asclepieion in Athens. In: Karl Kerényi: *Der göttliche Arzt. Studien über Asklepios u. seine Kultstätte.* Basel 1948, p. 72.

Fig. 23: Relief dedicated by Archinos to the oracle god Amphiaraos in Oropos (Attika), 380/370 B. C. In: Karl Kerényi: *Der göttliche Arzt. Studien über Asklepios und seine Kultstätte.* Basel 1948, p. 42.

Fig. 24: The sungod on his night journey, being protected by the Mehen serpent, and the overcoming of the Apophis (Apep) serpent, 7th hour of the Amduat, in the tomb of Thutmose III. In: Erik Hornung, Betsy M. Bryan (Eds.), *The Quest for Immortality, Treasures of Ancient Egypt.*, Fig. 16, p. 44.

Fig. 25: Regeneration in the serpent of time, 12th hour of the Amduat. In: Erik Hornung, *Das Grab Sethos' I/The tomb of Pharaoh Seti I.* Photos Harry Burton. Zürich, München 1991. Fig.2, p. 13.

Fig. 26: Hecate Triformis. Paris, Bibliothèque Nationale. In: Ives Bonnefoy, *Mythologies II,* Chicago, London 1991, p. 686.

Fig. 27: Ouroboros. Abraham Eleazar: *Donum Dei,* Erfurt 1735. In: Alexander Roob. *Das hermetische Museum. Alchemie und Mystik,* Köln 2006, p. 331.

Fig. 28: Athnasius Kircher: "Ars magna lucis", Amsterdam 1671. In: Alexander Roob: *Das hermetische Museum. Alchemie und Mystik,* Köln 2006, p. 71.

Fig. 29: Uräus snake with cow horns, 19. Dynasty. Valley of the Queens, tomb of Nefertari. Photo Jaques Livet. In: Philippe Germond, *Das Tier im Alten Aegypten,* München 2001, p. 177.

Fig. 30: C. G. Jung's tree in Bollingen. Photo of the author.

Fig. 31: Aion, mithraic, late Roman cult figure with key and/or staff as guardian to the afterworld, Musei Vaticani, Vatican, Italy.

Fig. 32: Goddess with snake. Ugarit, ca. 2500 B.C. In: Ives Bonnefoy, *Mythologies I,* Chicago, London 1991, p. 209.

Fig. 33: Brahmanaspati, 1916. The snake as symbol of the self in: *Das Rote Buch: Liber Novus* of C. G. Jung, facsimile edited and introduced by Sonu Shamdasani, Düsseldorf, London 2009, p. 54.

3. List of Dreams

Dream 1: On driving a car and the white cows
Dream 2: The little red cow in the water
Dream 3: The cow that gave birth
Dream 4: The statue of Hathor in the Museum of Ancient History
Dream 5: The ox-child

Dream 6: The two octopuses in the sea
Dream 7: The octopus / crab in prison

Dream 8: The black-and-white snake
Dream 9: The copper-colored snake
Dream 10: The child and the *Boa Constrictor*
Dream 11: "Cutting up" a snake
Dream 12: The captive snake
Dream 13: The "redeemer snake"
Dream 14: Snakes in the house
Dream 15: The green snakes in the pond
Dream 16: The rattlesnake entwined around the leg
Dream 17: A viper (common European viper) winds its way around me
Dream 18: The black cobra snake

4. Index

remark: name of gods, see under «god»
numbers, see under «number»
see a. = see also

– A –

Abt, Sabine 126
Abt, Theodor 76, 123, 126, 128, 130
Abt-Baechi, Regina 7, 11, 29, 50, 91, 102, 139, 142, 144
acceptance 44
achievement(s) / achieve 45, 64, 69, 73, 83, 156
Adam 25, 89, 128, 147
adaptation / adapt 10, 68, 69
adder, *see also snake* 89
adolescent 95
adrenaline 112, 113
advice 108
affect(s) 77, 95, 159
Africa 34, 109
aggression 158
aggressivity 116
Aion 128, 148
air / aer 55-6, 136
alchemist(s), *see also sages* 48, 54-6, 58-9, 83, 122, 128
alchemy 49, 54-8, 60, 75-6, 78, 92, 104, 122, 128, 147
– alchemical 49, 54-5, 75, 76, 156
alcohol 106
alien(ate)/ alienation 48, 70, 72, 147
alp / alpine 19-20, 133
ambiguity 98, 164
ambition 17, 83
ambivalence 26, 108, 118, 133, 161
Amduat, *see also Book of the Dead* 123-6, 130, 138
America, South 21
amplification(s) 10, 16, 41, 130, 142
analysis 80, 107, 114
ancestor 15, 70, 146, 159
anger 138
anima 17-9, 26, 79, 105, 150
animal(s), *see also adder; bee; behaviour; bull; cat(s); cattle; child, ox-; cobra; cow; crab; dog; donkey; fish; god; horse(s); insects; instinct; lion; octopus; rabbit; relationship; scarab; serpent; shark; snake; tiger; viper* 8, 10, 16, 19, 24, 27, 29-30, 34, 41, 51, 57, 59, 72, 82, 85, 94
– face / head of, *see a. face* 59, 63, 148
– help(er) of / dangerous 50, 84, 130
– like humans 30, 39
animus 17-19, 42, 59, 61, 82, 107, 109, 132
– and Mercurius 60
– creative principle 61
– negative 17, 22, 25-6, 40, 60, 62, 107
annoyance 17
Anthropos 57
anxiety 20, 119, 138
Apophis / Apep 123-5
apple(s) 23-25, 89, 142-3
archaic 21, 36, 41, 45, 122, 132, 153, 160
archetype / archetypal, *see also dreams; female; relationship; symbol; unconscious* 18, 26, 30, 35, 37-8, 41, 54, 58, 61-3, 74, 76, 78-80, 85, 96, 100-102, 116, 132, 140, 142-3, 147, 151, 155, 157-8, 164
– archetypal image 9, 26, 35, 106, 140, 144
– of feminine 40, 42
– of mother 38-40, 44
– of nature 52
– of renewal 63
– theory of archetypes 140
arm 69, 74, 77, 107, 156, 161
art / artist 42, 64, 136
assimilation / assimilate 106-7

associations 82, 111, 113, 140, 159
Athanasius 131
Atman 37
attachment, unattached 107
attention 33, 46, 52, 64, 83, 98, 101, 103, 120-1, 146, 163
attitude 29, 34, 37, 57, 60, 100, 135
– collective 78
– conscious 153
– false / wrong 18, 84, 136, 158
– ideal / sensible 113, 118
– new / realign / change 63-4, 154
– one-sided 37, 63, 148
– religious 102, 163
– towards unconscious / to life 61, 151
autonomy / autonomous 32-3, 96, 108
awareness 32, 42, 67, 84, 101, 114, 120, 146, 160

– B –
baby 27, 29, 32-3, 155
bee 122
Bächtold-Stäubli, Eduard 128
background, spiritual 58, 64, 129
bad, *see also evil; good* 116
balance 64, 97, 117
ball 34
ban 154
battle 74
beach 21-2
bear 50, 69
beauty 40, 89
bed(room) 102, 118-19, 155
behaviour / behave 10, 17, 30, 37, 54, 70, 71, 72, 84, 108, 160, 164
– instinctive / of animal 9, 36, 56
– right / not right 22, 26, 151
belief(s) 17, 41, 98, 121, 130, 136, 142
beyond (afterworld) 124
Bible 89, 95, 147, 159, 160
Birkhäuser-Oeri, Sibylle 20, 23
birth, *see also child; new, the* 26-7, 29-30, 33-4, 38, 53, 62, 128, 144, 156-8, 161, 163
– by / of cow 34, 35, 113
– divine 32, 159
– give / new(born) 27, 29, 33, 36, 156
black / blackness 23, 34, 81, 90, 92, 98, 104, 120, 126, 155-58, 161, 163
Bleek, Wilhelm H.I. 109
blessing 128, 133
blood 22, 77, 90, 98, 153
blue 22, 73
body 19, 30, 68, 71, 73, 103, 105, 107, 120, 125, 136-7, 140, 148, 154-56
– body and psyche, *see a. psyche* 109
Bollingen 145
book(s) 132
– about underworld, *see a. Amduat* 123
– Book of the Dead 123-6, 130, 138
– letters 163
– Red Book 162
boundaries 161
boy 44-6, 50-2, 57, 59, 62-3, 97-8, 100
brain 71
bread 91, 95
breath 84, 125
bridge 54, 80
Buddha / Buddhism 29, 32-4, 36-7, 62
bull 15-16
burial 23-4, 28, 123
bushmen (San) 109

– C –
calmness 15, 41
cancer 120
car 16, 17
care (n) 33, 63, 111, 114, 118, 153
career 18, 97
castle 23, 25
cat(s) 9-10, 91, 122
cattle 15, 19, 133
cave 16, 21, 23, 29, 91, 111, 113
Celtic 56, 128
central 37, 76
centre / central 32, 37, 76, 134, 147, 159
century 74, 98
– 16th 110
– 19th 19
– last 11
certainty / uncertainty 18, 98, 118
change 22, 24, 36, 46, 63, 69, 75-6, 84, 129, 132, 143, 148, 151, 153-4, 160
– image of feminine 114
– of attitude 94
chaos / chaotic 36, 76, 100, 105, 121, 133
character 40
chemistry 55
Chevalier, I. 73

child, *see also birth* 29-30, 33-4, 36, 44-6, 48-52, 57-8, 63, 89-92, 94-5, 100-102, 108-9, 140, 144
– and snake 91-2, 100-101
– as individuality 32
– childishness 32, 62-3
– children 32, 89-90, 92, 95, 100, 102, 118-9, 126, 130-1, 144
– divine 30, 62-3
– in puberty 95
– newborn 25, 26, 32
– ox- 44-5, 49, 51, 54, 56, 59-64, 104, 147
– young / old 32
Chinese 164
Christ, *see also god; Jesus* 29, 32, 58, 96, 139, 144
Christianity 25, 29, 38, 57, 60, 98, 151
– Christian(s) 33, 38-9, 41, 53, 60, 74, 78, 95, 98, 116, 139, 142, 144, 147, 150, 160-1
– Pre-Christian(s) 38
chthonic 46, 58, 105, 136
Church / ecclesiastical 54, 60, 74, 89, 98
circle(s, vicious) 133-4
clash, *see also conflict, opposites* 137
clothing 130
cobra 155-157, 159, 161, 163
coincidence / coinciding 71
cold (-blooded) 60, 90-91, 94, 130, 151
collaboration 113
collective, *see also attitude; individuality; relationship; unconscious* 19, 63, 78-9, 104, 108, 135, 147, 150 156-8, 164
– problem 54, 62, 113, 116, 150, 159
colour, *see black; blue; cow; green; red; yellow, white*
commitment 114
communication 130
community 147
compass, inner 36
compensation 54, 137
complement 10, 34, 122, 165
complex 21, 52, 70, 100, 109, 134
– mother 26
compulsions 97, 105
concentration 134
concept 37, 137
conception 34
condemnation 116
confidence 134
conflict 17, 82, 83, 121, 143, 164
confrontation 116, 132
Confucius 164
connection 45, 49, 50, 68, 71, 92, 142, 147, 148, 150, 153, 159, 164
– emotional 94
– reconnection 80
– to inner life 82
– to unconscious 135
consciousness / conscious, *see a. attitude; development; knowledge; life; unconscious* 9-10, 22, 30, 34, 46, 48, 49-53, 58-9, 61, 64, 72, 73, 76, 80, 83-4, 93, 98, 100-1, 103-4, 107-8, 113, 119-21, 124, 132, 135-7, 147, 150-1, 153, 157-8, 160-1, 163, 165
– approach / confront unconscious / nature spirit with 41, 50, 77
– arise in / from 116, 136
– become (not) 22, 24, 26, 30, 32, 36, 49, 52, 61, 92, 97, 103, 108, 123, 161, 164
– conscious viewpoint 137
– development / growth of 100-1, 122, 136, 147-8, 160
– dream compensates 79
– greater / higher 26
– light of 11, 36, 147, 161
– of men / male / of women 18, 59, 116
– principle of 78, 157
– renewal of 25, 123-4, 126
constrainment 24
constriction 25
contact 48, 70, 76, 140
context, *see also connection* 63, 109, 130
contrast 92, 139
control 32, 33, 89, 98, 101, 104, 137
conversation 80
conviction 17
cooperation 117
corpse 22, 111, 114, 116, 118
courage / courageous 121
cow, *see also goddess, Hathor* 7, 11, 14-20, 26-7, 29-31, 34-39, 41-2, 44, 52, 59, 61, 64-67, 71, 141, 155, 157
– companion of Great Mother 52
– divine 24, 36
– Earth-Cow 23-7, 29
– giving birth 53, 62, 113
– red / little 21-23, 26
– white 155-6, 160

crab 81-3
creation 25, 29, 42, 45, 106, 148
– act of / renewal of 29, 63, 102
– creative (work) 64, 74, 76, 102, 135
– creative problem / process 48, 79, 83-4, 98, 132
– creative spirit / force / energy 45-6, 51, 83, 135
– creativity / creative 8, 15, 26, 60, 61-63, 74, 76-7, 79-5, 83, 100, 102, 121, 133, 135, 138, 153, 161, 164
– creature 15, 69, 72, 74, 89, 94
– danger of unused creativity 82
– creation of world / universal creation 29, 106, 148, 163
criticism 51, 83, 136, 143
cross 50, 81, 96, 99, 139, 144
crown(s) 91, 92, 102
cruelty 103
cult(s) 98, 142, 148, 149
culture(s) / cultural 10, 15-6, 19, 21, 29-30, 35, 45, 54, 63, 78, 95, 102, 146, 156-7
– Christian 39, 41
– Western 33, 38, 137
custom 126, 133, 140, 160
cuttlefish 68, 74

– D –
damage / damaging 17, 60, 82, 131, 163
danger 16-8, 25, 30, 42, 58, 60, 63, 69, 73-4, 82-4, 89-90, 93, 96, 98, 101-2, 105-6, 108, 113-4, 116, 118-22, 124-5, 128, 130, 132-4, 136, 138, 140, 146-7, 150-1, 153-4, 157-9, 161, 164
dark(ness) 24-5, 36, 38-9, 55, 57, 61, 68, 73, 77, 81-3, 89, 91, 92, 98, 104-5, 119-20, 124-6, 130, 133, 139-40, 151, 159-61, 163
– dark side / god 25, 150-1, 160-1
death/ dead 25, 36, 39, 42, 73, 82, 102, 108-9, 111, 114, 118, 124-6, 128, 143, 146, 156-8
– and renewal 123
– dying 109, 114, 130
decay 63
defence / defense 82, 122
deity / deities, *see also god / goddess* 56, 98, 125, 163
– dark 159, 161, 163
– secret of 158
demand 40, 42, 121-2, 160
Democritus 122
demon(s) 54, 134, 146, 153, 158, 163
depression 17, 20, 23, 138, 151, 153, 158, 161
depth(s), *see a. depth psychology* 137, 155
desert 132-135
despair 62, 95, 161
destiny 30, 78, 79, 153
destruction / destructiveness 22, 40, 60, 63, 74, 109, 116, 126, 147, 157, 163
development, *see also consciousness; growth; process; women* 26, 71, 100, 107, 108, 137, 143, 158, 160
– evolution 70-72
– inner / psychic / spiritual 25, 48-9, 64, 98, 131, 143
– new 26, 63
– of consciousness 100, 136, 147
– threaten / hinder 26
– undeveloped 32
devil / devils, *see also Satan* 38, 55, 57, 60, 89, 120, 147, 161
– devilish / diabolical 57, 59, 74, 105, 137, 157
devotion / devoted 22, 61, 64, 160, 163
devouring 25, 39, 42, 84, 109, 122, 131, 151
diamond(s) eyes 90
difference, different 10-11, 19, 38, 40, 70-71, 124, 154
– male / female 60
difficulty / difficulties 61, 103, 133
disappearance 45
discovery 129
disease 92, 105-6, 119
dismemberment 24, 106
disorientation 83
disposition, common 39
dissociation / dissociated 9, 119
dissolution 58
distance 92, 95, 121, 131
disturbance 9, 26, 83, 94, 95
diver / diving 67-8, 77, 84
divine 8, 24, 29, 34, 53, 58, 76, 78-9, 128, 154, 158-9, 163
– and human 134-5
– child 30, 62-3, 101-2
– semi-divine 32
doctor(s) 109, 111, 113-4, 118, 139
dog(s) 9-10, 30, 69, 71, 94, 122, 132-3

dogma 54, 151
dominance 17, 157
donkey 30
door 44, 81-4, 118, 121, 158
doubt 52, 71
dove 150
dragon 104, 122, 128, 131
dream(s), *see a. consciousness; ego; image; symbol; understanding; women* 9-10, 16-8, 21-3, 26, 30, 34, 42, 44, 68, 72, 77, 81, 90, 92, 97, 111, 130, 134, 146, 155
– archetypal 10, 54, 58, 132, 147
– helpful / hint from 27, 139
– meaning of, *see a. interpretation* 16
dress 111
drive(nness) 16-18, 33, 76, 83, 96, 103, 160
– driving force, *see also instinct* 52
drug 106, 112
dwarf / dwarves 26, 46, 50, 62
dynamism 17, 40, 46, 109, 136, 137

– E –
earth 15, 39, 55, 57-8, 61, 105, 119-20, 133, 142-3, 150, 156, 159
Easter mass 89
East 33-34
eating / eat 25, 36, 69, 106-8, 129
Edda 142
effect(s) 11, 92, 143, 164
– enlivening / illuminating 80
egg 148
ego 61, 96, 134, 157-59, 161, 163
– dream- 151, 158
– egoism 22
Egypt(ian) 19, 30, 39, 43, 95, 123, 138, 156
– Ancient 30, 35, 38, 41-2, 106, 144, 147, 154
Eliade, Mircea 106, 144
emergency 63, 111, 113
emotion 18, 22, 45, 50-2, 59, 61, 63, 71, 77-81, 95, 100-101, 104, 124, 131, 134-6, 150-1, 158
empowerment 41
emptiness 69, 135, 161
enchantment, *see also witch; magic* 59
enemy / enemies 69, 74, 104
energy 17, 52, 79, 107, 133
– block / drain of / disappears 94, 97
– creative 46, 51, 83
– from unconscious / source of 80, 83
– life / psychic 62, 107, 137
enlightenment, *see a. light* 57, 92, 122, 130
enthusiasm 59
environment, inner 22
Epidaurus 138
equilibrium 18, 122, 165
eros / erotic 25, 42, 71, 116, 118, 133
eruption 153
Europe / European 24, 38
Eve 25, 89, 128, 147
evil, *see also bad; good* 21, 23, 25, 27, 57, 60, 62, 73-4, 84, 89-90, 92, 96, 98, 104, 130, 134, 146, 151, 157-9, 163
– and good 25
existence 18, 37, 40, 71, 118, 147, 151, 159
experience(s) 16, 33-4, 60-1, 64, 68, 74, 77, 82, 98, 106, 132, 137, 151, 153-4, 159
– of self 79
– singular / not sharable / hide 140, 154
expression 44, 53, 71, 108, 130-31, 138
extraversion / extraverted 40, 54, 83, 154
eye(s) 15, 21

– F –
face, ox 44, 46, 48, 50, 52, 63
fairy tale(s), *see also sagas; myth* 9, 16, 18, 23, 24-7, 29-30, 38, 41, 46, 50, 59, 62, 89-90, 100, 103-4, 109, 120, 140, 144, 146, 158
fame / famous 128
familiarity 42
family 95, 102, 131, 159, 160
fantasy / fantasies 37, 48, 50, 54, 61, 71, 77, 83, 97-8, 107, 121, 124, 134, 136
farmer / farming 146
fascination 67, 78, 138
fate 39, 46, 56, 128-30, 148, 159, 161, 164
father 23, 106-7, 109, 159
fear / frightening 73, 89, 91, 93, 98, 104-5, 108-9, 116, 119, 121-2, 130-2, 136, 138, 151, 155, 157-8, 161
feeling 15, 18, 23, 34, 40, 42, 45-6, 49-51, 53, 58, 61, 67, 77-80, 83, 89, 101, 107, 116, 137, 140, 151
felix culpa 24
female / femininity 17-8, 26, 35, 38-40, 42, 57, 60, 78-9, 82, 98, 111, 113, 116, 118, 125, 129, 132, 139, 142, 144, 147-8, 150-1, 156-7, 164

– female authority / magic 38
– female empowerment 41
– feminine nature / concept / image of 18, 25-6, 32, 40, 114, 116, 131
– principle / archetype of 40-2, 79, 116
– maternal female 25-7
– redemption by female 61
– feminism 41
– problem of feminine 18, 113-4, 116
fertility 29, 38, 41, 126, 128
fight 15, 41, 52, 59, 142
fire / fiery 22, 33, 56, 77, 91, 98, 122, 130, 160
fish 70, 91
flight 121
flood 124
folk, folklore 109, 144, 154
food 19-20, 27, 68, 108, 156
forbidden, the 158
forest 23-4, 26-7, 90-1, 119, 126, 130, 132, 140
fortune 92, 102
freedom 116, 151
freeze 36
friend(ship) 74, 118, 121
fright / frightening 89, 91, 109, 134
frustration 138
function(s), *see also anima; animus; intuition; thinking* 59, 71, 76, 82
– lower 103
– feeling 58
future 32, 34, 46, 59, 81, 90, 101, 109, 121, 128, 130

– G –
gender 42, 60
genius 44, 45
German(ic) 10, 23, 46-7, 98, 128, 142, 144
girl 77, 91, 106-7
Gnosis / Gnosticism 98, 139, 151
goal(s) 25, 27, 51, 76, 92, 120, 122, 135, 137, 157
god(s), *see also Buddha; chthonic; deity* 15, 25, 29, 32, 46, 56, 58, 60, 74-5, 78, 95, 124, 128, 147, 154, 157, 159-60, 163
– Aion 148-9
– ambivalent 89, 160
– snake- / serpent-gods 135, 138, 160
– animal (and human) 29-30, 148
– Apollo 144
god (cont.): Asclepius (healing) 114-5, 117, 138
– Christ/ Christian 32, 53
– creator / as creator 45, 148
– dactyls 46
– dark / evil / good god 57, 160-1, 163
– Eros 148
– Germanic 46-7, 144
– Greek 46, 57
– Indian 32
– Mercurius / Mercury / Hermes 56-63, 75, 147
– Mithras 148
– Norns 46
– Odin 144
– Osiris / Seth, Tammuz, Attis 106, 156
– Phanes 148
– redeemer 96
– Saturn 57
– Shiva 32
– sungod (Re) 36, 123-5, 147-8
– trinity 56, 98
– underworldy 56
– vegetation gods 156
– Yahweh 160
– Zeus 88
goddess(es) , *see also deity; Mary* 24-5, 29-30, 35, 56, 124, 144
– Aphrodite / Ishtar / Astarte / Atargatis 144, 150
– as cow / Hathor 19-20, 26, 30-1, 35, 37, 41-3, 59, 61, 144, 156
– death (Artemis, Kali) 112, 144
– Demeter 29
– Echidna 150
– Egyptian 35
– Eileithya 29
– Hecate 56, 127-8
– Iduna 25
– Indian 37, 157
– Isis 20, 35, 41, 43, 106, 144
– lower 156
– matronae / matres 56
– mother goddess 20, 29, 144, 151
– nature / tree goddess / of love 129, 144
– Nut, sky goddess 19, 35
– primordial 106
– snake 150, 154
– Sumerian-Babylonian / Semitic 144
– Thiamat 106

goddess (cont.): triple / of moon / fate (Brigit, moirs, norns) 128
gold(en) 21, 25, 34, 38, 42, 91, 154-6, 160
good, *see also bad; evil; opposites* 42, 57, 60, 68, 83, 89-90, 92-3, 100, 116, 119, 122, 124, 130, 142, 146, 151
– goodness 98, 160
Greece / Greek 29, 46, 56, 98, 104, 114, 128, 139, 148, 150
green, *see also snake* 22, 126, 131
grief, *see also sorrow* 20
Grimm, Jacob and Wilhelm 23
growth, *see also consciousness; spirit* 38, 79, 100, 128, 142-3, 156
– inner, *see a. development* 143, 157
guardian 149
guidance / guide(line) 33, 38, 79, 104, 124, 139
gut 89, 98, 137, 153

– H –
hair (curled) 44, 52, 55-6, 111
hand(s) 94, 97, 106, 109
Hannah, Barbara 10, 94, 117, 135, 153
harbour 17, 120
harm, *see also suffering* 107
harmony / harmonize 26, 100, 146
Hartmann, H. 102
head(s) 15, 30, 34-5, 48, 52, 56-7, 73, 91, 102-3, 113, 118, 125, 148
– cow 19
– three-headed, *see also goddess, triple; number three; trinity* 127
healer / healing 25, 38, 40-1, 58, 74, 92, 97, 108, 111, 113-4, 116-20, 122, 126, 138, 147, 151, 153
health 9, 112, 128
heart 77
help(er) 17, 24-5, 27, 38, 40, 62, 71, 90, 104, 113, 118, 121-2, 124-5, 130, 133-4, 137, 139, 154-5, 163-4
heresy 98
heritage 136, 146
hero / heroic 24, 26-7, 32, 38, 50, 59
heroine 23-4, 26-7, 38, 50, 59
hill 139
Hinduism 33, 137, 157
history, *see also idea* 29, 37, 60, 70, 73, 77-8, 104, 159
– ancient 37, 42
– historic(al) 90, 123, 151
– history of religion, *see a. religion* 16, 41
homeopathy 74, 122, 134
hood 44, 46, 49-50, 62
hope 126, 128, 157
horizon 34
horse(s) 10, 32
Hornung, Erik 89, 123, 126, 128, 150
hospital 114
hostility 101, 122, 124-5, 133, 151, 160
house(s) 23, 90, 118-9, 146
human (being) 11, 27, 29-30, 32, 39, 71, 73, 83, 122-3, 128, 142-3, 151
– and divine / partially human 30, 135
– beyond / not / super-human 29, 91, 103
– humanity / humankind 18, 29, 73-4, 89, 148
– human nature 29, 89, 146
humility 160

– I –
I Ching 37
Ibn Umail, Muhammad 76
idea(s), *see also inspiration* 16, 29, 34, 37, 42, 54, 71-2, 77, 80, 83, 84, 90, 94-5, 100, 104, 107, 114, 121, 124, 128, 136, 138-9, 142, 156-7, 164
identity 50, 78, 140
ideology 10, 53, 136
Iggdradsil 142, 144
illness 37, 106, 108, 120, 128, 151
– mental 58, 82, 104, 122
image(s), *see also archetype; change; female; mother; meaning; unconscious; women* 10, 16, 22, 24-6, 30, 35, 38-9, 48, 52, 54, 56, 64, 72, 75-6, 80, 100, 122, 125, 137
– brood upon 45
– create / creative 18, 51
– dream- 16, 26, 50-51, 134, 138
– inner 19, 45, 52, 68, 82
– harm 83
– understand 11, 48
imagination (active) 36, 45, 79, 84, 135-6
imitation 136
immortality 25, 123, 124, 125
impulse(s) 24, 48, 52, 61, 76, 78, 83, 98, 101, 107, 121, 150, 153
– creative / new 48, 77, 79, 83

impulse (cont.): dangerous / snake 113, 122
– from unconscious 94, 97
– helpful / healing / renewing 38, 58, 62, 104, 108 113
– instinctual / animal 59
inactivity 84
incubation 27, 138
independence 17, 25, 41
India / Indian 32, 155, 157
individuality / individual 22, 32, 41, 71, 80, 102, 116-7, 136, 146, 151, 153, 164
– individual and collective 164
– individual, significance of 147
individuation 143
inferiority 83
inflation 90, 154, 158
initiation 132, 153
initiative 76, 151
insanity 104
insecurity 18, 95
insects 136
inside, the 68, 69, 71, 82, 153, 159
insight 84, 92, 98, 120, 136, 153
inspiration, *see also idea* 83, 113
instinct(s), *see a. drive; knowledge; nature; processes; psyche; unconscious* 24, 33, 38, 55, 60-1, 96, 98, 101, 104, 134, 157, 163
– and restriction 160
– creative 153
– instinctive 9, 18, 23-4, 30, 36, 38, 41, 52, 59, 63, 89, 96, 101, 103, 113, 120, 161, 164
– instinctual 11, 56, 95-96, 113, 161
– instinctual basis / roots 93, 95
– instinctual nature 39, 52-3, 131
– maternal / feminine 24, 40, 156
– meaning of 120
intellect / intelligence 25-6, 33, 36, 49, 53, 68, 120-1, 134, 136-7
intention 30, 85, 107, 158
interest 71, 108, 122
interpretation 9, 42, 81, 158
– dream 9, 51, 58, 79-81, 92, 121, 140, 142, 155, 159
intervention 161
intolerance 116
introversion 33-4, 60, 77, 82-3
intuition(s) 34, 50, 71, 83
irrational 18, 52, 78, 89, 98, 100, 153
Islam 134
island(s) 21, 74, 154
Isler, Gotthilf 92, 102
isolation 108

– J / K –

Jaffé, Aniela 103, 150
jealousy 40
Jesus, *see also god; Christ* 32
Jew / Jewish (ritual) 155-6, 159-160, 163
Jung, Carl Gustav 8-11, 16-9, 30, 33, 36-9, 41, 46, 48-9, 51, 54-8, 60-2, 67, 71, 76, 78, 80-1, 84, 89-91, 93-6, 98, 103-4, 106-9, 114, 117, 119-22, 128-30, 134-7, 139, 142-45, 147-8, 150-1, 153, 157-60, 162-5
Jung, Emma 60
kill 25, 73-4, 91-2, 109, 113, 118, 156, 159
king 56, 78-9, 123
knowledge; *see also secret; spirit; nature; tree; unconscious* 11, 32, 25, 50, 59, 89, 92, 98, 104, 120, 124, 132-3, 144, 151, 157
– absolute / higher / spiritual 113, 120, 132
– ancient 32
– instinctive / irrational / nature- 9, 38, 98, 100, 113
– of unconscious / consciousness 34, 84, 113, 134
– secret 34, 114
– unknown 22, 26, 36-7, 42, 45, 49, 58, 60-61, 72, 103, 122, 133, 138

– L –

labyrinth 138, 142
lake 106
land 74, 78, 111, 146, 148
language 9-10, 24, 54-5, 80, 122, 165
Lanzckowski, G. 154
Lapidus, M. 154, 155
leader 153, 157
leaves 64, 118, 146
lecture 11, 132
left (direction) 16-7
leg 132-3
legend 16, 46, 62, 79, 89-92, 101-4, 107, 131, 135, 144, 146

life, *see also attitude; connection; energy; meaning; snake; spirit; tree; unconscious; water* 9, 16, 25-6, 36, 62-3, 69, 71, 73, 80, 84, 92, 101, 103, 109, 118, 121, 126, 128-9, 132, 134, 136, 142-4, 146, 150, 153, 156, 159-60, 163
– alienated from / stagnant 24, 161
– approach / attitude to(wards) 22, 61
– bring (back) / come to, see a. enrich 23, 25, 32, 77, 83-4, 113-4, 118, 133
– conscious / unconscious 48, 51, 59, 61
– cope with / demands of 17, 102, 143
– creative, inner / symbolic 42, 46, 51
– difficult / life problem 131, 155
– enrich / enhance / vivify / unfolding / renewal of 9, 17, 33, 37, 42, 46, 60
– eternal 148
– flow of / joy of 60, 79
– future of / spare 90, 156
– hostile to / threatening / without 82, 108, 130, 160
– new / give life 20-1, 24, 106, 131
light, *see also enlighten(ment)* 27, 34, 36, 84, 89, 95, 104, 120, 125, 130, 137, 139, 148, 150, 155, 160-61, 163
lion 10, 122, 148
logos 116, 156
loneliness 133
loss 40, 53, 54
love 18, 22, 25, 59, 77, 104, 112, 126, 129, 131, 132
– loving 40, 64, 140, 147, 160
– unconventional love 132

– M –
magic / magical 50, 114, 133-4
malice / malicious 60, 62, 140
mammal, *see also animals* 70
man, old (senex) 26-7, 40, 50, 57, 62
– male 17-8, 26, 39, 57, 60, 111, 118, 125, 156, 159
– masculine 17-8, 25, 40, 98, 107, 132, 156-8
Marduk 106
Mary / Virgin Mary 38, 78
mass 158
materia, materialism 54, 158
matter (substance) 48, 55, 98, 146, 158
– and spirit / spirit in matter 53-4, 105
meadow 89
meaning, *see a. dream* 80-1, 100, 120, 140
– meaningful / -less 10, 41, 80
– of life 60, 160
– of symbol / image 16, 94
mediator(s) 60, 150
medicine 106, 113-4, 118, 122
– medicine men 153, 161
meditation / meditator 27, 29, 32-4, 37
mediator 60, 150
Mediterranean 29
melancholy 45
memory 19, 77
metal 56
Middle Ages 96, 126, 139
milk 15, 23, 91, 92
mind 9, 15, 18, 25, 45, 49, 53, 69, 76, 92, 113, 134, 136
– mental(ly) 9, 18, 22, 36-7, 48, 60, 71, 120, 122, 150
miracle(s) 84
misery 15, 83
mistress 128, 150, 154
model, role 19, 40
money 22, 92
moon 56-7, 76, 128
moral(ity) / moralism 60, 103, 116
Moses 95-6
mother, *see also archetype of; complex; cow; female; goddess of; nature* 22-4, 26, 29, 38-39, 40-41, 44, 58, 91, 100-102, 114, 144, 146, 151
– archaic 21
– image 35, 38-9
– married 126
– mater 56, 158
– maternal 18, 20-7, 29-30, 32, 35-6, 38, 40-2, 52, 61, 113, 129, 144, 146-7, 158
– Mother Earth / Nature 25, 52, 57
– negative / stepmother, evil 23, 25, 38
motivation 11, 17, 36, 67, 83
mountain(s) 16, 24, 89, 100, 133, 140, 146, 154
multiplicity 96
murder 74
museum 37, 42
music 44-46, 79
mystery / mysteries / mystics 79, 98, 135, 138, 156
myth(s) / mythic 24, 30, 35, 58, 79, 90, 106, 123, 126, 128, 140, 147, 163

– mythology 18, 25, 30, 32, 36, 41, 50, 52, 62-3, 89, 91, 100-1, 103-4, 106, 109, 133, 140, 144, 150, 161

– N –

Narby, J. 114
nature, *see also neglect* 18, 24, 33, 38, 40, 42, 53-4, 58, 61, 68, 71-2, 76, 92, 96, 98, 118-20, 122, 126, 128-9, 143, 146-8, 150-1, 154, 160, 164
– ambivalent / twofold 104, 133
– creating order / balancing 36, 97, 122
– and humans / connect with / relate to 22, 41, 67, 90, 116, 151
– basis of 146, 150
– course of / nature process 34, 147
– creative / creativity from 36, 45-6
– dark / dangerous 42, 140, 150
– feminine / maternal / mother of, *see a. mother; female* 18, 24-6, 32, 36, 42, 52
– goddesses of, *see goddess*
– healing / helpful / renewal of 62, 97, 148
– human / god's 89
– inner / outer 9, 11, 22, 41, 42, 53, 68, 71, 135, 142, 146, 147, 151
– instinctive / instinctual / unconscious 11, 36, 39, 52-3, 131, 147
– knowledge from / of 38, 100, 151
– law of 143, 146
– of women 40
– protect 55, 153
– purposefulness of 52
– rejoices in / conquers natures 122
– spirit / wisdom (of) 27, 41, 53, 59, 64, 131, 137, 161
need(s) 69, 80, 97
neglect(ed) 60, 102, 140, 146-8, 150-3
nervous system 70-71, 103, 105, 136
neurosis / neurotic split 151
new, the 26-7, 32-3, 61-2, 63, 76-7, 83, 98, 101-2, 116, 121, 130, 153, 156-7
New Testament 160
night 91, 118-9, 121, 123-4, 139, 146
nourishment / nurturing 18, 23-4, 27, 33, 36, 42, 64, 156
number, *see also century*
– 2 (two) 16, 18, 50, 55-6, 68, 77, 79, 119, 126, 135, 144, 155, 158
– 3 (three), *see also goddess; head; triangle; trinity* 46, 50, 56-7, 113, 124, 126, 128-32, 140, 148
– 4 (four) 46, 76, 155
– 5 (five) 138
– 9 (nine) 144
– 12 (twelve) 124, 130
numinous, the 56, 58, 80, 158

– O / P –

obsession / obsessive 53, 109, 121
ocean 70
octopus 7, 11, 66-9, 70-6, 77-9, 81-85
odour, odourless 52, 55
one-sidedness 37, 40, 54, 63, 114, 116, 148
opinion 17-8, 22, 60, 108
opposites 10, 17, 19, 26, 56, 60, 62, 76, 78, 94, 101, 121, 143, 151, 156, 161
– divine 159
– reconcile / irreconcilable 51, 56, 143
– unify/ unite, *see a. unify* 51, 58, 137, 163
– pairs of / good-evil, male-female 55, 57
oppression 97, 121, 133
oracle 117
order 42, 76, 160
– create / meaningful 36, 53, 121
orientation / disorientation 76, 148
origin 45, 46, 56, 69, 119, 133, 135, 146, 163
Orpheus 46
ouroboros 128
ozone 44, 52, 55
pain 132
paint(ing) 79, 84
panic 131, 135-6, 151, 157-8
paradise 100, 144, 154
park 44, 49-51
passion(s) / passionate 39-40, 42, 151
patience / patient 63-4, 69, 84, 108, 111, 117-8, 122
pattern 24, 69, 142
peace 51, 18, 116, 154
people 18, 44, 68, 74, 76, 95, 122, 140
– archaic peoples / forest-dwellers 38, 132
– Nordic peoples 142
person(ality) 16, 19, 24, 30, 59, 69, 71, 82, 108, 134, 153-4
– feminine personality 131
– growth of / expand 49, 79
– individual / role of single 159, 164
– maturation of 118
– sick 134, 138
petrification 21
philosopher 76, 92

physicality 21, 36-7, 89, 98, 119-20, 122, 136
play / playful 51, 69, 76-7, 84
poison 10, 94, 97, 106, 112, 114, 121, 126, 134, 161
politics 18, 22, 42, 60, 63, 78, 137
pollution, inner 22
pond 21-2, 106, 113, 121, 126, 130, 132, 138
possession / possessed 24, 42, 157
possibility / -ies 30, 63, 77, 122, 130, 143
potential 32, 34, 52, 84, 131, 151
– creative 77, 82
poverty 9, 92
prayer 95, 133
pregnancy 33-4
prejudice(s) 22, 122
pressure 40, 44, 131
primordial 30, 32, 58, 106, 156
prince / princess 27, 50, 59, 77, 105
prison 81-4
processes(es), *see a. creation; nature* 97
– developmental / inner 48, 51
– instinctive / universal 24, 29, 36, 96
– unconscious / psychic 48, 51, 124
prohibition 158
projection(s) 21, 55, 74, 76, 105
prophecy 154
protection 22, 50, 125, 133-4, 157
psyche, *see also development; energy; process; unconscious; women* 10, 16, 18-9, 21-2, 24, 26, 29-30, 32-4, 52-4, 58, 67, 71-2, 76, 89, 97, 101, 103-4, 120, 126, 141-4, 147, 151, 157, 165
– and body / vegetative psyche 109, 119
– deep layer / level of 59, 108, 117, 138
– instinctual level of 56
– male / female (principle in) 18, 32, 39, 156
– psychic 51, 62, 82, 93, 114, 124, 130, 137, 156
– self-regulation / equilibrium of 32, 160, 165
– structure of 19, 41
psychologist, depth 67, 72
psychology 11, 17, 26, 71, 103, 140
– analytical / depth 18, 23, 26, 30, 41, 54, 58, 63, 71, 79, 120-1
– psychological 18, 41, 51, 134, 148
psychosis 158
psychopathology 103
puberty 97
puer aeternus 62-4, 102
purpose(fulness) 52-3

– Q / R –

queen 68, 77-9, 81, 102
rabbit 9
ratio(nality) / rational(ism), *see a. knowledge; irrational; thought* 9, 34, 36, 40, 51, 63, 122, 137, 148, 157, 159, 164-5
reality 18, 41-2, 98, 113, 121, 124, 163
realization 30, 81, 161
– realize 10, 18, 25, 40, 52, 84, 122, 156
reason / reasonable 38, 45, 51, 82, 98, 113, 121, 130, 136, 158, 163-4
– reasoning 33, 89
rebirth 38, 143, 151
recognition 83
– recognize 19, 23, 25, 36, 51, 53, 68-9, 77, 84, 94, 147, 157, 160-1
red 21-3, 26, 68, 69, 77
redeemer / redemption 21, 59, 61, 89, 93, 96, 102-3, 111, 113, 138-9
reflection 102
regeneration 125
regression 26
regulation (by unconscious) 37
rejection 80, 121
relationship(s) 15, 25-6, 40, 42, 46, 61, 63, 67, 69, 72, 109, 116, 126, 132-3, 143, 146, 156-7
– archetypal / personal 80
– destruction / loss of 40, 60, 107
– relatedness 18, 25-6, 151
– to animals / nature / other 50, 84, 116, 151
– to animus 61
– to feminine / women 25, 57
– to the collective 164
– to unconscious 18, 50, 52, 101-2, 163
religion 33, 146, 157, 159-60
– history of / loss of, *see a. history* 16, 41, 53
– pagan 142
– religious, *see also attitude* 10, 30, 32, 53, 60, 63, 98, 160, 163
– religious system 37, 157, 161
remedy 114

renewal / renew 9, 22, 24-5, 32, 41, 59-60, 62-3, 75, 98, 102, 106, 114, 118, 123-6, 130-1, 138, 143, 147-8, 151, 159, 161
– blocking / dangers of 63, 124
repression 63, 116
rescue 154, 164
research 11, 67, 71
reservation 109, 111
resistance / repulsion 109
respect 17, 26, 81, 122, 165
responsibility 22, 101, 163, 164
restlessness 20
restriction 24, 160
resurrection 126, 156
resuscitation 111-3, 118
retreat 24, 50-1, 122
reverence 53
revival 114
rigidness 40, 91, 160-61
ring 133
risk 73
ritual(s) 40-1, 156, 159, 163
– rite 130, 132
road 16, 17, 49, 78, 129, 146
rock, *see also stone* 74
Roman(s) 96, 115, 149
root(s) 142-3, 151, 163
rules 21
Russians 21
ruthlessness 129

– S –
sagas 18
sage(s) 32, 34, 62
sarcophagi 123
Satan, *see also devil* 159-60
saviour, *see also redeemer* 96, 104, 154, 157
scarab beetle 124
Schweizer-(Vüllers), Andreas / Regine 89, 98, 126, 150
science(s)/ scientist 54, 67, 70, 74, 121, 157
sea 61, 68-9, 74, 77
seal 161
secret 34, 39, 91, 108, 118, 128, 158
– in matter / nature 42, 54
– secret knowledge 130
seduction 25, 39, 60, 147
self, *see also king / queen; experience; psyche; relationship; snake* 32, 37, 76, 78-9, 81, 84, 94, 121-2, 133-4, 161-2
– self-confident 26
– self-destructiveness 109
– self-renewal 62
– self-sacrifice 24, 40
sensitivity, sensitive 116
separation 70
serpent, *see also snake, ouroboros* 25, 56, 89, 92, 95, 102, 104, 111, 121, 124-5, 128-9, 135, 137, 139, 147-8, 150-51
– alchemical serpens, *see a. snake* 156
– and unconscious 102
– appease / worship 98
– birth of 163
– chthonic 105, 136
– fiery 95
– guiding 139
– Kundalini 137
– Mehen / Apophis / Apep 123
– of salvation / sōtėr 96
sexuality / sexual 17, 56, 74, 95, 131, 155
shadow 22, 39-40, 52, 62, 76, 133, 158
shaman(s) / shamanistic 38, 153
shark 69, 74-5
ship 72, 154
shoe(s) 100, 102
significance 11, 30, 49, 56, 90, 142-3, 158
sin 10, 89
skin 95, 119, 138, 148
sky 19, 123, 136, 142
sleep / sleeping 106, 119, 121
smell, *see a. odour* 34, 44, 55-6, 71
snake, *see also redeemer, serpent, viper* 7, 10-11, 89-98, 100-9, 111-4, 117-8, 120-4, 128-135, 138-140, 146-148, 150-7, 159, 164-5
– Aesculapian 113
– ambivalent / twofold / mercurial 89-90, 97, 104, 108, 119, 133
– and death / light 104, 109, 111
– and divine / of life 98, 154-5
– and god (gold) / self 94, 154, 161-2
– and staff 114, 121, 149
– and time(s) / of time 125, 131
– and tree / woman 142
– as gut-thinking 153

snake (cont.): biting / dangerous / devouring / threatening 94, 108-9, 122, 126, 132, 136, 150, 156, 161
– black, *see a. snake, white* 126, 158-59, 161
– Boa 100
– cobra(s) 155-9
– coiled / embracing / wrapping around 106, 137, 151, 154
– copper / bronze 94-5, 97, 121
– creative / and creation / renewal 100, 102
– cross adder 140
– crucified / on the cross 139
– cutting 106, 109
– earthy 136
– encircling / embracing 134, 153
– feeding 23, 84, 91-2
– green (dark) 113, 126, 132
– healing / helpful / medicine 97, 111, 113-4, 116, 118-9, 122, 155
– hostile / evil 133, 151
– intention of 137
– kiss 103, 135
– Mercurius as / serpens mercurii *see a. god, Mercury* 104-5, 120, 147
– poison(ous) / venom / kill(ing) 97, 102-3, 105, 109, 113, 116, 118-9, 122, 154
– rattlesnake 132, 135, 138
– rescue / rescuing 116-7, 154, 164
– shedding of skin / molt 138, 148
– spiritual side of / spirit of 104, 120, 136, 138, 148, 163
– trapped / captured / chasing 107, 155
– Uraeus snake 105, 125, 141
– white 90, 92, 118, 120-1, 130
society (-ies) / social 18, 22, 41, 54, 59-60, 78, 84, 117, 137, 147, 153, 164
solution(s) 46, 62, 71, 97, 119, 135, 138, 153
son 23, 26, 44, 49-50, 57, 100-1, 105
sorrow, *see also grief* 138
soul 23, 45, 49, 54, 58, 95, 109, 150-51
– ancient / deep layers of 36, 107
– emerging from 90
– guide 104, 139
– healing of / redemption of 41, 59
– reality of 23, 143
– structure of the 18
source, *see also spring* 19, 42
South Africa 67, 70
spirit(s), *see also development, soul, potential, principle, reality, snake, unconscious, value, view, woman, world* 15, 26, 57, 63, 71, 73-5, 79, 93, 96, 98, 128, 133, 148
– and knowledge / guiding 33-4, 120, 132
– and unconscious / forming symbols 36, 40, 60, 104, 135-6, 138, 148
– autonomous / superior 32-3
– chthonic 105
– concept / understanding of 58, 104, 136
– creative 8, 51
– dark / evil / devilish 60, 134, 137, 163
– divine / holy / overpowering 53, 126, 163
– enriching / vivifying 60-1
– intellectual / masculine / rigid 40, 53, 59
– life-promoting / helpful 37, 42
– nature / of matter / of substance / Mercurius 27, 41, 53-4, 56, 58-9, 64, 137
– new / old / traditional 32, 59, 63
– ordering / origin of 37
– spiritual, *see a. values,* 22, 25, 27, 32-4, 38, 42, 55, 58-9, 61, 71, 98, 104, 120, 122, 129-30, 132, 142, 146, 150, 153, 165
– spiritual forces / principle 33, 41, 146
– spiritual life 60, 150
– spiritual roots 142
spirituality 98, 120, 139
split 9, 106
spontaneity, spontaneous 30, 32, 62, 69, 71, 75, 90, 95, 98, 100-1
spring(s), *see a. source* 128, 139, 143, 150
squid 68, 73-4
stairs / staircase 44, 49-50
stars 19, 35
statue(s) 27-9, 23-3, 37-8, 42, 62, 115
stone 56, 76, 92, 140
– lapis lazuli 154
– philosopher's (*lapis philosophorum*) 92, 122
Storl, D. 40
story / stories 9, 23, 25, 30, 50, 72, 74, 81, 92, 100, 146, 154, 161
stranger 90
stream 128
struggle 135
subjectivity / subjective 97
success / succeed 40, 49, 62, 82, 103, 118, 157
suffering 40, 46, 48, 50, 58, 61-3, 82-3, 112
suggestion 49, 59, 121, 128, 158

suicide 108
sulphur 44, 52, 55-6, 59
sun 36-7, 55-6, 124, 140, 148
– disk 19, 26, 30, 35-6, 42, 54, 59-60, 123, 125
surprise / surprised 21, 90, 104
swallowed, being 48, 73, 128
swim / swimming 111, 126
Switzerland / Swiss 19, 20, 77-9, 102, 144
symbol 9-10, 25-6, 29-30, 32, 41, 67, 74, 76, 90, 92, 94, 104, 133, 162
– ambiguous 58
– ancient / new 22, 164
– archetypal 10, 62, 78-9, 85, 96, 100, 102, 116, 151
– dream 9, 23, 54, 140
– inexhaustible 90
– number symbolism 46
– significance / importance of 9, 90
– symbolic 9-10, 23, 30, 37, 41, 48, 72, 54, 74, 76, 78, 96
– symbolism 45, 50, 100, 104, 119, 133
– understand 48, 54, 55
symptom(s) 36, 105, 151
synchronicity / synchronistic 164

– T –
tail 23, 128
task 61, 112, 122-3, 153, 159-161, 164
temple 28
temptation 80
tenderness 44
tension 44, 46, 48, 50, 61, 63
terror 112, 138
thank(fullness) 154
theory, psychological 139
therapy 109, 134
thinking 16, 27, 34, 36, 40, 98, 136-7
– gut 151, 153
thirst 134
thought(s) 9, 16, 19, 30, 34, 48-9, 74, 82, 97, 107, 121, 133-4, 147, 153
– rational 40
– right 164
threat / threaten 24, 26, 73, 76, 84, 89, 92, 97, 108, 114, 117, 122, 131, 133-4, 137-8, 146, 153-4, 157-8, 161, 164
threshold 58
tiger 52
time(s) 17, 69, 74, 128, 148
– and snake / as serpent 128-9
– flow of 46
– modern 10-11, 63, 116-7, 138, 146, 157-8
– passage of 128
– problem 62
– timelessness 143
tomb 39, 110, 123, 141, 144
tongue 130
oneness, *see also unity* 96, 164
tradition / traditional (s) 32, 89-90, 114, 116, 122, 128, 140, 146, 148, 155, 157
transformation 26, 29, 38, 48-9, 92, 117-8, 124-6, 130, 138-9, 143, 148, 151, 156, 160
transition 95, 98, 130
trauma 22
treasure 27, 103-4, 118, 130
treatment 116, 134
tree(s) 23-25, 41, 89, 140, 142-6, 150, 156-7
– and birth / children / maternal 144, 147
– apple / growth / of knowledge / life 142-4
– deciduous 139, 143
– leafless / old 142, 155
– world tree 142
triangle, *see a. number three* 44, 50, 52, 55-6
tribe 35, 38, 153
trinity, *see god(s), trinity*
trust 69, 97, 107, 151
truth 53, 108

– U / V –
unconscious, *see also autonomy* 9-11, 18, 20-4, 27, 33, 36, 45-6, 49-51, 58-64, 71, 73, 75-9, 81-4, 90, 92, 95, 97-8, 100-3, 107-9, 113, 116, 118-20, 122, 124, 128, 132-4, 136, 138-9, 142, 146-8, 156, 159, 161
– and conscious(ness) / attitude / behaviour / relationship towards 18, 22, 26, 33, 49-50, 58, 60, 100, 116, 130, 137, 150-1, 163
– and symbol / symbols of 58, 108, 140
– archetypal structure of 116, 124, 155
– collective 18, 35, 52, 63, 116, 119, 124, 138, 150, 156
– connection (to) / within 49, 63, 67, 135
– creation by / creative 46, 51, 81, 164

unconscious (cont.): danger / dark/ threat / harm (from) 17, 26, 93, 102, 105, 114, 122, 138, 140, 151, 157-8, 161
– depth / deep level of unconsciousness 30, 79, 93, 103, 120, 132
– emerge / grow from 32-4, 46, 50-2, 77, 83, 93, 121, 131
– image from / of 24, 48, 51, 126
– instinctive (realm of) / instinct(s) 11, 34, 97, 107, 134, 161, 164
– intention / interest of / purpose by 107, 151
– knowledge of / wisdom 62, 134
– life / light / energy from 26, 83, 101, 130
– female / masculine, *see also anima* 17, 59
– maternal 23, 26, 34, 52, 158
– new / healing / impulses from 29, 32, 48, 62, 94, 97, 108, 113-4, 126, 153
– overwhelming by 158
– personal 22, 119
– background of 9-10, 19, 26, 32, 36, 40, 67, 78, 103, 113, 123, 132, 147, 155
– spirit of 26, 40, 53, 60, 104, 135, 136, 138
– unconsciousness 147, 148, 158
– wants to be realised in life 61
understanding, *see also image; unconscious, spirit; symbol* 9, 11, 29, 52-4, 80, 108, 116, 138, 140, 161
– dream, *see also interpretation* 27
– symbol / symbolic language 23, 54
underworld / underground 37-8, 56, 123-5, 128, 130, 147
unification / union, *see also opposites* 22, 25-6, 51, 56, 58, 79, 96, 134, 137, 139
– unity / unify, *see a. oneness* 56, 95, 121
– uniformity 117
urgency 119
value(s) 22, 33, 41, 62, 78, 63, 148
– feeling 79, 80, 116
– feminine, spiritual 42, 79, 151
vessel(s) 146, 163
viper, common, *see also snake* 139
vision(s) 53-4, 107, 161
vivifying 22, 32-3, 61
voice 45, 156, 158
von Franz, Marie-Louise 9, 17-9, 23, 30, 32, 36-7, 41-2, 46, 50-1, 53-4, 57-60, 62-3, 76, 78-80, 82, 90-1, 101-2, 104-7, 109, 111, 116, 119-120, 126, 128, 134, 136, 139-40, 143-4, 146, 156, 158-9, 161, 164
vulnerability / vulnerable 83, 100

– W / Y –
wall 118, 119
war 21, 63, 84, 102, 116, 135, 136
warmth 22, 24, 42, 77, 118
warning 15, 17, 89, 103, 118, 122, 131, 137, 147, 153, 157
waste 21-2, 91
water(s) 21-4, 26, 33, 56, 68, 79, 81, 84, 95, 106, 108, 111, 113, 119, 126, 140
– no 133
– of life 134
wealth 36, 72, 92, 102, 142
Western, psychology / standpoint 34
wheat 155, 156, 160
white 16-18, 27, 34, 90, 92, 98, 104, 120, 126, 130, 156, 160
wholeness 32, 40, 76
wild 52, 68, 69, 148
wind 45, 55, 56
wisdom, *see a. snake* 26, 32, 34, 38, 40, 62, 98, 100, 104-5, 119, 121, 130, 135, 137-9, 144, 161
– (of) nature 120, 131, 137
– wise person 27, 29, 33, 38
witch 27, 38
witness 158, 161
woman / women, *see also female; mother* 16-18, 24-7, 34-5, 37-42, 44, 52, 59, 77, 79, 82, 102, 107, 109, 111, 114, 131, 139-40, 142, 144, 146, 150, 155-6, 159
– aged / old 24, 38, 111, 114
– dreamer 20, 26-7, 32, 34, 38, 42, 68, 94, 108
– equal right of 41
– image / role of 40, 114, 116
– pregnant 29, 33-4, 144, 155
– relation to feminity / animus 60
– spiritual development 25
– unconscious / psyche of 97-8
– young 25, 101, 118, 132-33, 159
womb 29
work(ing) 21-2, 102, 108, 135, 143
world view 30, 53, 54
– modern / Western 21, 29, 41, 148, 151
– outside world 33-4, 68, 82, 165
worship 29, 98, 142
yellow 55
youth, *see a. woman, young* 25, 95, 97, 109